Anonymous

Her Majesty's Prisons

Their Effects And Defects. Vol. II

Anonymous

Her Majesty's Prisons
Their Effects And Defects. Vol. II

ISBN/EAN: 9783744752701

Printed in Europe, USA, Canada, Australia, Japan

Cover: Foto ©ninafisch / pixelio.de

More available books at **www.hansebooks.com**

HER MAJESTY'S PRISONS:
THEIR EFFECTS AND DEFECTS.
VOL. II.

LONDON:
PRINTED BY GILBERT AND RIVINGTON, LIMITED,
ST. JOHN'S SQUARE.

HER MAJESTY'S PRISONS:

THEIR

EFFECTS AND DEFECTS.

BY ONE WHO HAS TRIED THEM.

IN TWO VOLUMES.

VOL. II.

London:
SAMPSON LOW, MARSTON, SEARLE, & RIVINGTON
CROWN BUILDINGS, 188, FLEET STREET.
1881.

HER MAJESTY'S PRISONS:
THEIR EFFECTS AND DEFECTS.

MALE WARDERS are divided into four grades—chief warders, principal warders, warders, and assistant warders; of these, of course, the billet of chief warder is by far the most important, so we will give him the priority due to his rank. The work of chief warder, if conscientiously carried out, is probably the most responsible and difficult of any of the prison officials. If anything goes wrong, he is the man that gets all the blame; and when things go smoothly and well, the governor gets the thanks. During the absence of the governor the chief warder acts as deputy governor; and as all the prison business passes through his hands, it is necessary that he should be a pretty fair scholar. In addition to this it is requisite that he should be a man of the strictest integrity and a first-rate disciplinarian, for, standing as he does between the governor and the warders, everything depends upon the latter thoroughly respecting their chief, and feeling sure that any breach of regulations will not be glossed over by him.

The warders are only (excepting in very rare cases) fined or reprimanded at the recommendation of the chief warder, and their applications for leave have all to be signed and approved by him before they are presented to the governor. It is therefore of the last importance that the chief should carry out his duties in the most straightforward manner, for any infringement of the regulations or illicit practices would inevitably place him in the power of some or other of the warders, to the great detriment of discipline and good order. Under the Government scale the pay of chief warder has been considerably increased, but when one has really seen and considered the arduous and responsible nature of their work, I very much doubt whether the authorities can obtain the class of men they require, even at the advanced salaries they now offer.

The prisons are divided into a first and second class according to their size, and it is a common, and as far as I can judge pretty correct complaint, that the first class prisons get anything they require, while the second class are left to pig along as best they can. At the former, the chief warders get 150*l.* per annum, and a house and uniform. At the latter, the salary commences at 100*l.* per annum, house and uniform, and rises by yearly increments of 2*l.* to 120*l.* At the Xshire Prison (which is rated as second class) the chief warder under the county got 80*l.* per annum, with house, fuel, light, uniform, and boots. In this arrangement the second class prisons certainly went to the wall, for before the Government took the prisons the salaries of chief warders were all much the same (80*l.* a year being an exceptionally high one); but here there was only an immediate gain of 20*l.* per annum, while at others the salary was just upon doubled.

The chief warder's work commences at six o'clock in the morning and terminates at ten o'clock at night, the consequence being that he is obliged to get up every morning at 5.30, and never gets to bed until eleven. He is not of course on duty the whole time, for no man could stand such continual labour as that, but his work is divided as follows:—His quarters are always within the prison walls, and he must be at the prison doors at six o'clock in the morning to unlock them and allow the warders to enter and commence their duties. He must then go round and unlock the various other exits of the prison, as all doors are locked overnight by his master-key, and once this is done, no one but himself or the governor can get into the prison. He is then at liberty to return to his quarters again until eight o'clock if he chooses; but as a matter of fact the time is generally spent in looking over the night reports, seeing the men started at the treadwheel, and the various other work that he is unable to find time for during the day's routine. At eight o'clock he has to be in the governor's office awaiting the arrival of the latter, and after going over the night reports, attends him as he goes his daily round of inspection. This completed, he sees the men pass down to their morning turn of treadwheel, and then applies himself to the various office work he has to do, and at the Xshire Prison this was considerable, for he had the entire management of the supplies needed for the mat-making carried on in the prison, and the disposal of the mats when made. He has the examining and approving of all stores sent to the prison; and no food of any kind is supposed to enter the prison without having been first seen by him. At 11.30 he has to be in chapel to see the men come in, and that over, has to go down to the governor's office and assist him in meting out the punishments incurred by prisoners for breaches of the rules during the previous day. His afternoons are just as fully taken up, and, in addition to his regular duties, the moment anything goes wrong, the immediate cry is, "Send for the chief." At six o'clock in the evening he goes round and puts the master-key upon all the out-buildings, and upon all exits from the prison, with the exception of the main door. He is now free to go where he pleases till ten o'clock, subject, of course, to the chance of being sent for at any moment; but at that hour he must be back to go round all the prison building, male and female, and see that all exits are duly fastened with the master-key, and to finally lock the main door, leaving the night watchmen safely locked up inside the prison. If anything happens during the night, however, he is the man that is roused, as there is a bell communicating between the prison and the chief's quarters, that the night watchman rings in case of any disturbance, or sudden illness, amongst the prisoners. One hundred sovereigns can hardly be considered an exorbitant price to pay for the satisfactory performance of such a multitudinous collection of duties as I have enumerated above, and I hardly understand how competent men can be got to do it at the price. I have heard it hinted, however, that there are various pulls to be got out of the food contracts, which form a very pleasant addition to the regulation 100*l.* a year. "A good master makes a good servant," and the old saying holds good in the prison service as elsewhere.

At Z—— Prison, Captain K—— was a model governor, and the chief warder was a capital officer, keeping the warders firmly in hand, and allowing no departure from the rules and regulations upon any excuse whatever. Having served as a non-commissioned officer in the Army, he knew exactly what discipline meant and how to manage the numerous old soldiers he had under his command.

At Xshire the governor was lax, and knew next to nothing about his work, and the chief was more than proportionately remiss. He had the great disadvantage of having been a civilian all his life, and consequently had never had any experience in governing men, and with a lot of old soldiers under him, who were up to every move on the board, he was completely outmatched. He was a most pleasant man to speak to, and an easy-going, good-natured kind of fellow, but was utterly wanting in moral courage. This was the worst feature about him, for if he saw a warder breaking the rules, he was afraid to go up and give him a sharp reprimand, but instead of that he would walk off and tell the cook that he saw So-and-so doing what he had no business to be doing; then the cook would tell the engineer, the engineer would pass it on to somebody else, and finally it would come to the ears of the offending warder. Even if the governor, by any rare chance, happened to come into the prison, an event which occurred once in six months, and discovered any breach of the regulations, the chief would always try and find some excuse for the warder, and persuade the governor not to fine him. This was mainly owing to the fact that the chief was engaged in some very questionable proceedings inside the prison, and was afraid, if he offended any of the warders, that a hint would be given to the authorities. The natural consequence of this was that all kinds of abuses sprang up in the prison, and the warders did pretty well what seemed good in their own eyes. The Government rules and regulations will never be properly carried out, and abuses will invariably creep in till the authorities offer higher pay, and can induce a superior class of men to accept these appointments. Even then there ought to be stringent supervision of the stores supplied to the cook, and an occasional unexpected examination of the quantity of food he was actually making. In the same way examinations ought to be made of the articles supplied by the different contractors, so that the authorities might be quite certain that the goods really were what the chief warder and contractor represented them to be. Otherwise, an inferior article might be supplied, and the two pocket the difference.

Principal warders come next in rank, but are only employed in the very large prisons, where they do a lot of supervision work, such as seeing the men told off for the treadwheel, &c.; that is done by the chief warder in smaller prisons. Their pay commences at 85*l.* a year and rises to 100*l.*; but as we did not have any of them at Xshire, I know very little about them.

We now come to the warders and assistant warders, comprising a considerable body of men—1246—and upon whose integrity and respectability the reformation of the criminal in a great measure depends. Their number has been considerably increased by Government, and their pay nearly doubled.

Under the county a warder's pay commenced at 15s. a week, and rose by yearly increments of 1l. a year until it reached 50l. per annum, at which sum it stopped. In addition to their pay they received a house, fuel, light, uniform, and boots.

Under Government the pay of an assistant warder commences at 60l. a year (23s. a week), and rises 1l. a year till it reaches 65l. per annum (25s. a week). Warders commence at 70l. a year and rise in the same way to 75l., each receiving house and uniform, but no fuel, light, or boots.

Under the old system they were all (with the exception of the last appointed man) called warders; now there are only a certain number of warders at each prison, according to the size of it, and the rest are all styled assistant warders, the promotion being by seniority.

At Xshire we had two full warders, Humphrey and old Bob, although there was a serious dispute as to the latter's right to the billet as Rugby had been three months' longer in the prison service. It would seem that they both applied at the same time for the billet of assistant warder, and that Rugby was accepted and the other rejected, both however having so many testimonials that it was a very even question which the magistrates should select. Three months later the magistrates found that they would require a new receiving and hospital warder, and as they had been very well satisfied with old Bob's testimonials, they sent and offered him the billet, so as to save the trouble of again advertising the appointment for fresh competition. Rugby was of course at this time the last-joined officer, and accordingly styled assistant warder, while the man undertaking the duties of receiving and hospital warder had invariably been appointed as warder, and styled so; and the consequence was that Bob had been called warder some four or five months longer than Rugby, although the latter had really seen three months' longer service.

Under the county, Rugby always ranked as the senior, and as it made no pecuniary difference, nobody said anything about it. When the prisons changed hands, and it was discovered that the two senior warders only would be styled warders, and receive an extra 10*l*. a year, old Bob immediately put in his claim, though I believe he only did it as a try on, and without any real hopes of his claim being allowed. Fortunately for him, however, he had been a marine, and as the new governor was a marine, and the Government Inspector had also been in the same service, they both stood by Bob when the matter was referred to them, and ousted Rugby, who had been a soldier. It was a very unfair thing to do, and I do not think the matter would have ended here, had not Humphrey, at the time, decided to retire on his pension, and Rugby, knowing that he would get the vacant billet, thought it better to keep quiet.

I have entered rather fully into this matter as Rugby was not fairly treated, and there was a very strong feeling about the matter amongst the warders, and as it helps to explain why the governor was so much disliked, and distrusted by the warders.

The pay of a warder now is very fair, as wages go, and the Government, if they took the trouble, could get really competent, respectable men. Unfortunately, although there has been an elaborate list of the requisite good qualities to be desired in a man applying for prison warderships drawn up by the framers of the Prisons' Bill, the instructions are continually neglected, and some *protégé* of the governor or chief warder is smuggled into the billet quite regardless of what his antecedents may have been. There is so much fuss, letter-writing, and interviewing before a man can obtain an assistant wardership that one would naturally suppose, if one were not a little behind the scenes, that it would be impossible for any one but a man with unblemished character to obtain the situation; but when one knows that this is simply so much silly formal red-tapeism, and not the slightest barrier to an utterly worthless scoundrel being appointed if he only has a friend at court, the matter becomes too serious for joking. Now there is not the least exaggeration in this statement, although at first sight it may seem hardly credible.

There is at the present moment a warder in H.M. convict establishment at P—— who was dismissed from the Xshire Prison for gross misconduct, and so bad was the record against him that although he had served for nearly twenty years under the county (and his long service was earnestly pleaded in his behalf for some mitigated form of punishment) the magistrates declined to alter their decision. Notwithstanding all this the man had not been three months dismissed before he was appointed warder at ——. Now here is proof positive of what the regulations respecting these appointments are really worth, when one comes to the practical working of them. Here was a man, totally unfit for the billet, bundled in without the slightest inquiry concerning his previous career, simply because he happened to have a nephew a clerk in the office of Mr. T———r clerk of the works to one of the large convict establishments, and this clerk induced Mr. T———r to use his influence to get the man appointed. It would, I suppose, have been well-nigh impossible to have found a worse man for the work; he was a bad-tempered, lying, unscrupulous scoundrel, and in addition to the breaches of discipline the magistrates dismissed him for, he had been accustomed for years to levy black mail on the prisoners in his corridor, obliging them to give him a certain percentage, and a pretty large one to, of the small sum they were enabled to earn in the prison.

It would be a great improvement if Government would issue a regulation that all applicants for assistant warderships must have previously been non-commissioned officers in the regular army, and have completed at least twelve years' service at the time of making the application. This would insure men being employed who were accustomed to having others under their command, and who would know exactly what discipline was, and how to enforce it. It would also insure their being a certain age, a most desirable regulation, as there is no greater mistake than to get young men of two or three and twenty, and give them almost unlimited control over a large number of prisoners.

It is the greatest possible mistake to employ marines; they are most unsuited for the work, are nearly always given to drink, invariably use foul language, are rough and inhuman, and, in addition, are regarded with contempt by both the naval and military prisoners. I do not know why this should be the case, but I do know that it is so, and wherever there is any particularly unpopular warder in a prison, it is a hundred to one he is a marine. This was fully borne out by my experience at Xshire; there we had two on the regular staff, Bob and the gate porter, and another, Podgers, who was employed temporarily. Of these Bob (it's of no use mincing the matter) was a most unscrupulous, inhuman old brute, and would drink and swear as much as two ordinary men. The gate porter was detested by both warders and prisoners, while Podgers was a thorough bad lot in every way.

The authorities can perfectly well afford to pick and choose, as there are always a large number of applicants whenever there is a vacancy; and when one remembers the very great power that is placed in the hands of warders, the public have a right to demand some guarantee of fitness for the post, and past respectability of character in those who obtain the situations.

There are numerous and constant cases of gross cruelty and injustice in our prisons, and many a prisoner's life is lost by the neglect and ill-treatment of brutal warders. A man in prison has no opportunity of bringing his grievances before the notice of the authorities, for the monthly visit of the Government Inspector is a silly farce, and whether prisoners are treated fairly or not depends entirely on the warders; at all events it did at Xshire, and I expect it is the same in all but a few of the prisons where there are exceptionally clever, conscientious governors.

To show that I am fairly justified in making this statement I will just mention one case out of many that came under my own immediate observation. While I was at Xshire, an old watchmaker, undergoing a sentence of three months' hard labour, was transferred to us from another prison, and placed on arrival in A ward, where Podgers, who was employed temporarily during the summer, was acting as corridor warder. I do not know what the old fellow was sent to prison for, but presume he was sentenced by one of the great unpaid, for he ought to have been sent to an asylum not a prison. Podgers, like a cowardly scoundrel, seeing that the old man was of weak intellect, immediately selected him as a safe and amusing subject for bullying and ill-treating. A very little worrying would throw the poor old chap into a fury of excitement and he would shout and scream at the top of his voice. This used to delight Podgers, who was always inventing some new torment for him. One of his favourite tricks was to turn the old man's gas down so low that he could hardly see, and as the old fellow had bad sight, and was very fond of reading, this was a great annoyance to him. Whenever Podgers was on duty of a night, the whole evening was spent in shouting and screaming, while when the other warders were on duty, the old chap would be as quiet as possible. One day the old man arrived in chapel with a bad black eye and a cut nose, and this aroused my curiosity, and I determined to find out what Podgers was doing to the old fellow. Whenever I had made any inquiries before, I had always been told that the old chap was cracked, and made a noise about nothing; but I now felt sure that however great a lunatic he might be, he was not likely to go punching his own head. I accordingly set to work and got hold of one of the prison staff, from whom I could always get any information I wanted by a little judicious flattery, and after a slight cross-examination this was the account he gave me.

It seems the old watchmaker had a habit of walking up and down his cell, and while engaged in this monotonous employment, used frequently to stop just opposite the door and stand lost in meditation for a quarter of an hour and sometimes twenty minutes at a time. God only knows what piteous aching thoughts passed through his mind, or what strange scenes or fancies, perhaps, presented themselves to the poor tangled brain as the old man stood thus gazing into vacancy. Goaded nearly to raving madness by a constant system of petty annoyances, he was, perhaps, looking forward with an intensity of heart-sick longing that it would be impossible to imagine, to the day when his sentence would be ended, and he could once more go forth a free man. Be this as it may, Podgers discovered this trick of the old man's, and immediately saw a new way of ill-treating him without the slightest danger of getting himself into trouble. His *modus operandi* was as follows : he used to creep quietly along the corridor till he reached the old man's door, and then peeping through the spy-hole, see whether he was standing in his accustomed position; if he was, Podgers used to slip the key quietly into the door, gently turn back the lock, then suddenly dash the door open with all his might, striking the poor old watchmaker a violent blow on the face with the iron-lined surface of the door, and sending him flying to the other end of the cell. The old chap had a habit of stooping his head rather forward, and this quite accounted for the state of his eye and nose. Podgers could indulge in this pleasing amusement with a moral certainty of immunity from blame as he could always say that he did not know the old man was standing there, and that as the door stuck a little, he was obliged to use some force to get it open. As a matter of fact, I do not believe that there were any questions asked, for when the old watchmaker commenced a complaint to the governor, as he was going his rounds, about his eye and nose having been hurt, the governor walked straight past his cell and declined to take the slightest notice of him or his complaint, and as soon as the governor had completed his rounds Podgers went back to the old man's cell and pointed out to him the utter uselessness of making any complaints, and threatened him with divers pains and penalties for having had the impudence to attempt to make one.

Now I do not for a moment mean to assert that all prison governors are as grossly and dishonourably negligent of their duties as Major S—— was on this occasion, but the possibility of such a thing occurring shows how important it is that Government should do their best to obtain thoroughly respectable, trustworthy men for prison warders, as this would be the best and surest way of preventing such cases of ill-treatment as I have here mentioned.

Under the county system the warders were allowed, on application to the governor, to have work done for them or their families by the prisoners.

For instance, there were nearly always two or three tailors and shoemakers in the prison, and a certain portion of their time was placed at the disposal of the warders, and they could thus get clothes and boots made for themselves or their children at the simple cash price of the material. In addition to this there was a large piece of spare land within the prison walls that was divided into gardens for the officials, from the governor downwards, and each warder was allowed a prisoner to cultivate his plot of garden. The magistrates used to reckon up all these privileges as part of the emolument enjoyed by the warders, and hence it was that they got such low money payments. It was a very smart idea, for of course there was not sufficient work to be done for the prisoners to keep two or three skilled tailors employed, and the consequence would have been that some of the tailor prisoners would have had nothing to do if it had not been for this arrangement. The Government stopped all this kind of thing when they took the prisons, and passed a stringent rule forbidding the prisoners being employed at any kind of work for the warders. This would, at first, appear to be a very wise and salutary regulation, and were the prisons properly carried on, and the various rules strictly enforced, I have no doubt it would be extremely beneficial. At present, however, this regulation is invariably broken, and the warders have their things made and mended by the prisoners, to the very great prejudice of discipline and good order.

The prisoners are perfectly well aware that the warders have no business to be giving them private work to do, and of course only do what is required, on the understanding that they are to have some extra food, or some other indulgence. It would be far better if Government would reintroduce the old county rule, and let certain days be allotted in each week on which to allow warders to employ prisoners. This would put an end to all favouritism, and they might save a considerable sum by docking the pay of all warders a couple of shillings a week, in consideration of allowing them this privilege. While I was at Xshire there was a first-rate tailor doing eighteen months' hard labour there, and this fellow was kept busily employed every day from six to eight in the morning, and from five to eight in the evening, doing private work for the warders. In consideration of this the warders persuaded the doctor to order this man eight ounces of cooked beef every day; cocoa and white bread in lieu of porridge and brown bread; and an extra hour's exercise every day, and, in addition to this, used to give the man tea and cake, and half a dozen other little things. It was just the same thing with the shoemaker, there was a regular shoemaker's shop down in the receiving ward, and here there was always a man employed, or rather supposed to be so, in mending the prisoner's shoes, bed straps, or any other leather work or mending that required to be done.

As a matter of fact, however, like the tailor, half his time was spent in doing work for the warders. It was the same story all through, and the carpenter, blacksmith, and cooper, were all doing the same thing.

After I had been a short time at the prison I could always tell whether the governor was away for the day or afternoon; if he was, there was sure to be three or four prisoners busily working away in the warders' gardens. Of course, if the chief warder had been doing his duty this would have been out of the question; but for him to have interfered would have been a regular case of the pot calling the kettle black, and so things went on in this extremely confidential kind of way. If the regulations are not going to be strictly enforced it would be far better, as I have suggested above, to do away with them. The warders are now well paid, though I am bound to say they are fearfully overworked in the smaller prisons, but I believe in the large establishments, where they keep up a sufficient staff, the work is light enough. The magistrates invariably cut things down as fine as they could, yet, under their rule, three more warders were employed at Xshire than there are at present, although the number of prisoners then was far smaller than it is now. This increase of prisoners is caused by the Government having greatly reduced the number of local prisons, and being obliged to keep those they have filled right up in order to have sufficient accommodation. To do this they send prisoners about from all parts of England, whereas, under the county system, each county looked after its own criminals, and simply received the men that were convicted of crimes committed within its own limits.

At Xshire, under the county, the daily average number of male prisoners was about sixty-three; under Government it is about a hundred and twenty, yet, to meet this large increase in the number of prisoners, the staff of warders has been reduced. The natural consequence of this was, of course, that the warders had to work pretty well night and day. Humphrey proved to me that he had done a hundred and four hours' work one week, and the following week it increased to one hundred and eight hours. This was an average of over fifteen hours a day, and when one remembers the kind of work it is, the unflagging attention, and the never-ceasing vigilance it requires, the constant tax there is upon the brain, and that, in addition, nearly the whole of this fifteen hours was passed in standing or walking about, it will easily be understood how fearfully hard the work is.

The minimum daily average at Xshire, exclusive of Sunday, was thirteen hours a day, and any warder away on leave, or travelling with prisoners, or employed in any other way that prevented his being at the prison, increased the work for those who were left.

They commenced duty every morning, winter and summer, at six o'clock. Three days a week they went off duty at six in the evening, and the other three days they had to stop till ten o'clock at night. Sundays they came on duty at seven a.m., and stayed till four p.m. on two Sundays in the month; the third Sunday they were on duty from seven a.m. till ten p.m., and the fourth they had for themselves, and did not come on duty at all. The work was far too severe, and the warders were sometimes so completely worn out before their day's duties were over that they were quite incapable of properly carrying out the discipline of the prison.

At the Z—— Prison (and I believe at all other prisons) the cook had to take his turn at evening duty, and this considerably lessened the weekly number of six a.m. to ten p.m.

days that each warder had to do; but at Xshire the governor refused to allow the cook to do any duty, although the warders pointed out that cooks had to take their turn at other prisons.

The fact was, the cook did all the private baking for the governor's family for nothing, and, in addition, assisted the chief warder to make a very comfortable thing out of the stores; consequently both the governor and chief took uncommon good care that he should not be asked to do anything he did not like. When men are harassed and overworked, they naturally become ill-tempered and disagreeable, and the unfortunate prisoner has, of course, to bear the brunt of it. We luckily had, with a few notable exceptions, a wonderfully decent set of warders at Xshire, and, as they all understood each other, and pulled well together, things went on far better than one could have expected.

Still, this is not the kind of happy-go-lucky way in which Government institutions ought to be carried on, and the sooner the commissioners can be taught that it takes just as many warders to look after a hundred prisoners as it does after a couple of hundred, the better it will be for all concerned. Above all, let the authorities introduce some system by which the antecedents of all men applying for warderships may undergo an impartial and minute examination. At present any man that can ingratiate himself with the governor of a prison can always get placed on the prison staff, no matter what his previous character has been. This was notably the case with Podgers; he had been a marine, and used to run after Major Street, touching his cap and bowing down before him, and the consequence was that directly an order came down from the commissioners that an extra man was to be taken on as temporary warder, Street immediately sent for Podgers, though, if there had been any impartial examination into the character he bore in the place he would never have been selected.

This man, Podgers, was actually drawing Government pay from no less than three different sources, and only doing work for one.

He was drawing a pension of about 14s. a week; his pay, as sergeant on the militia staff, was about 1l. a week, and his pay as warder 23s. a week, so that altogether he was doing pretty well, and if ever Government had a bad bargain they had one in him. Still, for this one black sheep there were plenty of other good men and true, and, on the whole, I feel sure that we had a far more decent set of warders than the authorities had any right to expect, considering the careless manner in which they select them. I must not forget, however, that every single warder, with the exception of Podgers, had been selected and appointed by the magistrates while the prison was still under the county, so it was really no thanks to the commissioners that the warders were a decent lot, for their only nominee (Podgers) was most decidedly not a happy selection.

The female warders are a very small body compared with the males, and under Government their number has only been slightly increased, but their scale of pay has been considerably augmented. Under the county they commenced at 25*l*. per annum, and rose to 40*l*., not, however, rising by regular yearly increments, but only as vacancies occurred. For instance, under the county, there was a matron at 50*l*. a year, a deputy matron at 40*l*., a warder at 35*l*., another at 30*l*., and an assistant warder at 25*l*. The pay would remain at exactly the same figure, no mattter how many years they were there, unless one of the number died or retired. If the matron died or retired, of course all hands got a move; but if, say, the warder at 35*l*. a year retired, then the one at 30*l*. took her place and scale of pay, the assistant moved up to 30*l*., and a new assistant warder was taken on at 25*l*. In addition to their pay they were allowed quarters in the prison, light and fuel, uniform and boots. The uniform consisted of a long blue cloth cloak and black straw hat trimmed with blue for outdoor wear, and grey alpaca dress, with white apron and key bag, for their indoor duties.

Under Government their pay is 40*l*. a year for assistant warders, 45*l*. for warders, 50*l*. for deputy-matrons, and 55*l*. for matrons. At large prisons a much higher salary is paid to the matron, and a superior class of person is employed, but small prisons like Xshire have no regular matron, only a senior warder as acting matron.

In old days it was the women who had been ladies' maids and upper housemaids in the big country-houses that usually got these appointments. They were generally widows who had married the coachman or gardener, and being left unprovided for by his untimely decease, their old master, who was sure to be a county magistrate, used to look out for the first vacant billet as warder for them in the county prison. They are thoroughly unsuited for the work, for they no sooner find themselves with a lot of prisoners under their thumb than they immediately want to play at being fine ladies.

There is not the slightest doubt that the state of the female prisons was just about as bad as it could be when Government took the prisons over, and whether they have done anything to improve that condition is more than doubtful;

at all events they had not at Xshire, and the state of things there was, if possible, slightly worse than before.

At Z—— things were equally bad; but when Captain K—— got there he quietly informed the matron and the warders that he meant to have the Government regulations strictly carried out, and to see personally that they were obeyed to the letter—warning them at the same time that any breach of discipline would bring down prompt punishment on the head of the offender. They foolishly imagined that Captain K——, like other governors, was accustomed to talk very big and do very little, for they went on with their old tricks—having friends into the prison to see them, and committing other little breaches of the regulations, according to ancient custom. They quickly found, however, that they had made a huge mistake in their man, for not a thing was done within the prison that he did not know or hear of, and in less than six months he had cleared out the whole of the old staff of female warders and installed an entirely new lot.

There is such a demand for employment among the middle-classes that I am sure there would be no difficulty in obtaining quite a superior class of persons for these appointments, if the Commissioners would only take the trouble to try, and could manage to introduce the new state of things *en masse*. It would not, of course, do to attempt any kind of amalgamation, or the proverbial "Kilkenny cats" would be nothing to the fighting that would go on. If the nature of the employment was properly explained to the class I have suggested, they would be only too glad to accept the appointments, and the work would be no harder, and infinitely preferable, I should imagine, than that required of a nursery governess, or even of a governess in many middle-class families. For those who wanted an object in life there would be a wide field open for the employment of all their energies, and great and lasting good might be done among the outcasts of society by women who would throw their whole heart into the work, and earnestly strive to deserve in the great hereafter the gentle words of loving commendation, "In prison and ye visited Me."

The "male other sub-officers" mentioned in the list consist of cooks, engineers, messengers, and gate porters. Their number has been greatly reduced, but the increase of salary more than counterbalances the reduction. A cook's salary under the county was 50*l*. a year, house, fuel, and light. Under Government they get 75*l*. per annum, house, and uniform. The engineer under the county got 50*l*. a year, house, fuel, light, uniform, and boots; under Government he ranks as a principal warder, and receives a salary of 80*l*. a year, rising by yearly increments of a pound to 85*l*., with house and uniform.

Engineer is an imposing kind of appellation, and how he ever got the name heaven only knows, as a prison engineer knows about as much about engineering as he does about Greek. He is nominally supposed to be a kind of Jack-of-all-trades, to be competent to superintend any carpentering, building, draining, blacksmithing, or any other kind of work that may be going on in the prison. In addition to this he has to understand gas-fitting and plumbers' work, to see also to the heating of the prison in winter, and to manage the steam boiler, by means of which all the food is cooked.

These appointments, while the prisons were under the county, were made in the usual happy-go-lucky kind of manner that generally characterizes the proceedings of the great unpaid, and the engineer at Xshire was no exception to the rule. He had been apprenticed to a gas-fitter and plumber, and after serving his time continued to work for the same master. In this capacity he was sent up to the prison to thoroughly overhaul the water-taps and gas-fittings of the various cells. This was necessarily a longish job, and kept him knocking about the prison for several weeks, during which time he had ample opportunity of ingratiating himself with the governor and getting to know all the dodges of the place; and the man who at that time was engineer happening to die suddenly, Perth (such was his name), the gas-fitter, applied for the vacant billet, and having been employed about the prison for some time, the magistrates decided to take him on. How they could conceive that an uneducated young man of this description was a fit and proper person to place in charge of the heating, ventilating, and general sanitary arrangements of the prison I do not pretend to know; but there he was when I arrived, and for all I know to the contrary he is still doing his best to poison prisoners with bad air in the summer, and freeze them to death in the winter.

The arrangement for the ventilation of the cells was perfect, so far as it went, and provided always that the engineer carried out his instructions. In the centre of the end wall of each cell there was a moveable iron ventilator that communicated directly with the outside air, and which secured a constant and steady supply of pure air. Over the top of the door and exactly opposite to this ventilator there was a long, narrow, perforated iron grating, which communicated with the tunnel that ran the whole length of the corridor, and which was supposed to collect the foul air from all the cells and pour it into the main air-shaft, from whence it was expelled into the open air. This foul air was, of course, to be drawn along the tunnel by keeping a fire lighted in the shaft and creating a vacuum. Had the instructions for this purpose been properly followed the prison would have been perfectly ventilated; but Perth was either too lazy to see that the shaft fire was kept lighted, or else supplied his own house with the coals he was supposed to be burning there. I believe the latter theory was the true one.

In addition to the state of the cells there was no adequate means of escape for the foul air that collected in the central hall of the prison, and the smell there of a morning was enough to knock you down, and the first thing the warders did when they came on duty was to open the large door leading out to the exercise-ground, and so give the place a thorough good blow. I complained of the state of things to the chaplain, to my corridor warder, to the doctor, the engineer himself, and finally to the Government inspector, Captain L——, but without the slightest result. I laid the matter before Captain L—— when he came round on his monthly visit, and his answer was,—

"Well, I am afraid we cannot help you."

The chief warder on this occasion was extremely fine. I pointed out to Captain L—— that instead of there being a steady draught out through the escapement ventilator, there was actually a slight flow of air into the cell from it. The chief thereupon tried to persuade me (and did, I believe, persuade Captain L——) that this was the hot-air grating, and not the escapement one. I could not help laughing, for, in addition to thoroughly understanding the theory of the thing, I had gone over the whole practical working of the existing arrangements with both the engineer and the chaplain. It was, however, a good enough yarn for the inspector and governor, and I could get nothing done. I afterwards discussed the matter with the chief, and he frankly owned that he knew I was right. The water-tanks were equally neglected, and the water we had to drink was for some time more than half mud, and totally unfit for human consumption. I complained about it to all hands, and finally drew the doctor's attention to it.

"Ah, yes, to be sure—to be sure," he said; "the filters are all out of order. I mentioned it to the governor about a month ago, and it's going to be seen to."

I collapsed at this and gave the matter up as hopeless, for I naturally concluded that if the doctor had told the governor a month before, and they were only still " going to see about it," nothing I could say would have much effect.

It was just the same story with the heating of the prison; it was never properly attended to, and the water would be boiling away in the pipes at the head of the corridor, while the cells at the opposite end would be cold as ice. This kind of thing is very annoying, and still more so when one remembers that a staff of presumably competent men are appointed by the Government and paid high salaries to visit the various prisons at regular intervals and satisfy themselves that the ventilating, heating, and general sanitary arrangements are in a thoroughly efficient and satisfactory condition.

One of these gentlemen, Captain Mac'Hardy, came down to the prison while I was there; but as they knew the day on which he was coming three days beforehand, I need scarcely say that all the fires were burning merrily when he arrived, and that everything was ship-shape. Perth was always in fear and trembling when Mac'Hardy came down, for the latter was well up to his work, and asked the most awkward questions; questions which Perth, knowing nothing whatever of his work, was at his wits' end how to answer. When Campbell or Cameron came down it was all right, for they were equally ignorant of their duties, and Perth could bounce them, but when Mac'Hardy was there Perth crawled along in the rear with a most sheepish appearance. In order to correct any mistaken impression that might arise, let me at once say that I know nothing whatever of either Mr. Campbell or Mr. Cameron, and for aught I know to the contrary they may be exceedingly clever and competent gentlemen. I have simply repeated what I heard from the warders, and what I know was said by Perth. It is a pity that Captain Mac'Hardy does not manage to slip down to one or two prisons without advertising his arrival two or three days beforehand, and then I fancy he would get his eyes open a little.

Messenger warders are employed, as their name denotes, in carrying the various messages that pass between the prison and the town, and in going to and fro to the post-office to receive and deliver the letters. Their pay under the old system was just the same as any other warder, and under Government it has been increased in the same proportion. Piggot, the messenger warder at Xshire, was a capital little fellow, and I have already referred to him pretty often, as he had charge of me while I was awaiting trial. His office was no sinecure, for in addition to going some five or six times a day to the town he had to see to the cleaning and arranging of the various offices of the prison, and was debtors' warder into the bargain. One way and another he was going all day and every day from six o'clock in the morning till nine o'clock at night. Here let me say a word for the poor debtors. They are usually young fellows with affiliation orders against them that they are unable to pay, or small tradesmen who either cannot or will not pay their debts. Their number is also sometimes swelled by men who are bound over to keep the peace and cannot find sureties. Their place of confinement is entirely apart from the criminal portion of the prison, and they are permitted to associate together, and to wear their own clothes. If they have money they are allowed to provide their own food, and when this is the case they can manage to pass away the month or two which is usually the extent of their sentence pretty comfortably. It is here that the new imprisonment for debt laws so utterly break down, for the man who really deserves to be made uncomfortable, that is to say, who can pay and will not, really suffers only a very trifling inconvenience, for he can provide himself with every delicacy of the season if he chooses, and can have in a fair quantity of wine or beer into the bargain. On the other hand the unhappy debtor who really cannot pay because he has no money in the world to pay with, and who, consequently, has no means of providing himself with any extra sustenance, undergoes considerable privations, for the Government allowance of food is totally inadequate, and any one caring to test the following dietary can easily and quickly prove this to his own satisfaction :—

Dietary for Debtors.

Breakfast and Supper.

Bread 6 oz.
Gruel 1 pint.

Dinner.

Bread 4 oz. Potatoes 6 oz. Suet pudding 4 oz.	Sunday and Wednesday.
Bread 6 oz. Potatoes 8 oz. Cooked beef 3 oz. (without bone).	Monday and Friday.
Bread 6 oz. Potatoes 6 oz.	Tuesday, Thursday, and Saturday.

Men when they have been on this diet for about a month are ready to eat their shoes, and to keep men on it for three months at a stretch, as is frequently the case, is positive barbarity. Under the county their dietary was scanty enough, but it was a considerable improvement on the above, and the least Government might do would be to return to it:—

Dietary for Debtors under the County.

Breakfast and Supper.
Gruel 1 pint.
Bread 8 oz.

Dinner for Four Days.
Dressed meat 3 oz.
Potatoes 1 lb.
Bread 8 oz.

Dinner for Three Days.
Soup 1 pint.
Potatoes 1 lb.
Bread 8 oz.

I do not think even the most hard-hearted creditor would consider that this diet was on too sumptuous a scale, and the increase of expense to Government would be very trifling.

Gate porters under the county were on the same scale of pay as any other warder, but under Government they are placed on a higher scale, receiving 70*l.* a year, rising by yearly increments of 1*l.* to 75*l.* per annum. They have nothing whatever to do with the prisoners

—with the exception of having a prisoner out three or four times a week to clean up the gate and gateway—so it does not much matter what sort of fellows they are, but, as a rule, they bear the name of being a very ill-tempered lot, and certainly the man at Xshire was a most surly, vile-tempered, ill-conditioned curmudgeon.

Female clerks, Scripture readers, lady super-intendents, and "female other sub-officers" I know nothing whatever about, but presume that their pay has gone up on a proportionate scale with the other members of the prison staff.

I have now finished the list of officials, and given as well as I could some slight idea of their duties and the way they performed them. I think we may safely conclude that the Government staff is on a far more expensive scale than the old county one, and that until a more careful system of supervision is established, and greater trouble taken in selecting competent men, there can be no proportionate gain in efficiency.

In the meantime we had been hurrying along in the mail-train, and were rapidly drawing near the end of our journey. Some dinner had been brought from Z—— for us, consisting of half a pound of bread and a good-sized hunk of Australian beef each, but the travelling had made me ill and feverish, and I did not care to eat. The schoolmaster had a small sum of money belonging to me, and I asked him if I might get a bottle of seltzer water or something of that kind for myself, but he told me that it was impossible as the money would have to be handed over to the governor of the Xshire Prison, and be kept by him until my discharge. Early in the afternoon we arrived at the Xshire station and found Watergate, the chief warder, awaiting our arrival. An omnibus was also in attendance to take us up to the prison, and the dragoon and myself with our escort got inside, while Watergate, mounting the box, took his seat beside the driver, and away we went at a good pace and soon reached our destination. Once more I found myself in front of the gloomy portals of the Xshire Prison, and after the usual preliminary bell-ringing and parleying we were admitted by the gate porter who greeted the schoolmaster and Pell with a condescending urbanity that was a treat to behold. Once safely within the prison-gates the schoolmaster produced the key of our handcuffs, and unfastening them handed us formally over to the custody of the Xshire chief warder. The arrival-bell was rung, and in a few minutes Old Bob came puffing up the hill, and ordering us to follow him, led the way down to the receiving-ward. Unlocking a cell-door at the head of the ward he ordered the dragoon to enter, and shutting the door upon him conducted me to a cell a little lower down, and, with the information that he would come and see to me presently, carefully locked the cell-door and hurried off. Tired out by the journey, I seated myself on the stool, and resting my arms upon the table wearily laid my head upon them and tried vainly to conjecture how I should get through the twelve long months that lay before me. I had already done eight days of my sentence, for the time is calculated from the day the assizes commence, not from the day you are convicted, and as the assizes had begun on the Monday, while my trial did not take place till the Saturday, I had, as it were, gained five days; still there were 358 days more to do (it was leap year), and oh, what a time it seemed to look forward to! My meditations were interrupted by the sharp click of the trap-door as it was cautiously opened, and turning round I saw a grinning face stuck in the aperture, while the small portion of red and grey cap that I was enabled to see told me that it was one of the prisoners who had managed somehow or other to unfasten my trap-door. After another introductory grin, the fellow said in a hurried whisper,—

"Hie, governor, have you got a bit of baccy?"

"I have not got any," I replied.

"Oh, all right," he answered; and after a moment's hesitation was commencing to ask me some further questions when, I suppose, the sound of some approaching footsteps warned him somebody was coming, for he hastily closed my trap and disappeared.

I puzzled my brains for some time wondering how the fellow managed to open the trap-door, but could not make it out, as I knew all the traps shut with a strong spring-lock. I afterwards found out that the prisoners employed in cleaning the prison used to look out for a thin nail, and by bending the point up in a particular way were enabled to open any trap-door.

Shortly after, this trap episode, the cell-door was unlocked, and the cook entered carrying a newspaper parcel in his hand which he laid upon the table saying, " Here is the dinner they brought from Z—— for you; I heard you couldn't eat it on the way, but you had better try and tackle it now."

He was a smart-looking little chap, with a very long beard, and from the careful way in which he had it curled and pulled out, and the caressing manner in which he was continually stroking it, coupled with my after-experience of his cooking, I fancy he bestowed a considerable deal more attention upon this hirsute appendage than upon studying the mysteries of the culinary art. As a matter of fact his knowledge of cookery was of the very slenderest description, he having been brought up as a clerk, and started in life in this employment. Marrying young, and the care of a family coming quickly upon him, he found the slender salary he could command as a clerk totally insufficient for his wants, and determined to try his hand at something else. He had some claim upon one of the county magistrates, and this worthy justice, under the impression, I presume, that any one could cook, obtained the billet of cook to the county prison for him. Here, then, for the last four or five years he had been trying his 'prentice hand upon the provisions of the unfortunate prisoners, and, notwithstanding this somewhat long novitiate, I can, from bitter personal experience, fairly and impartially declare that I do not believe a man with less idea of cooking could be produced, search " the wide world o'er." It is, perhaps, unnecessary to add that this appointment was made while the prison was under the county authorities.

On the departure of the cook I came to the

conclusion that his advice was good, and determined to try and eat a little of the dinner provided for me, and, proving the truth of the old adage that " *L'appétit vient en mangeant,*" I got through all the beef, and the best part of the bread. I had not long finished my repast when Old Bob bustled in with his arms full of clothes, and, throwing the bundle down on the floor, said, " There are your things; now get into 'em as quick as you can, and then I'll come along and put up your own clothing in the portmanteau, and then it can be locked, sealed, and put by till you want to go away again."

I proceeded to examine the clothing Old Bob had brought, and found the number and quality of the articles to be pretty well the same as at Z——, with the exception of the suit here being of a dark grey colour and the cap and stock of the same. It was altogether a far more Christian combination than the Z—— chocolate and brown uniforms, and as all the prisoners, civil, naval, and military, were at this time dressed alike, they presented a less fantastic appearance than my late companions. The only distinction made here was that felons had a narrow red band running round the centre of their caps.

With lingering regret I once more cast aside my civilized apparel, gave a parting brush to my hair, and had barely completed my toilette ere Old Bob came puffing and fussing in with an armful of shoes.

"What kind of sized shoe do you take? I don't suppose we have any small enough, but you must just find the best fit you can out of this lot."

With these words he dropped the collection of old shoes he was carrying, and hurried off, leaving me to fit myself as best I could.

Old Bob was in a fine fluster; he had several men to change, I expect, as I could hear him puffing and blowing, and spitting and cursing, and hurrying from one end of the corridor to the other, while the entertainment was periodically varied by his shouting and swearing at his cleaner, or some unfortunate new-comer.

I searched about amongst the collection of old and new shoes that the old chap had left on my floor, but finding nothing that would at all fit me, finally selected a pair of new shoes (for the reason that they were new) several sizes too big for me, and having slipped my feet into them commenced folding up my own clothes ready for packing when Bob returned.

Every man on admission is supposed to be placed in a cold bath, but whenever Bob had much to do, rules and regulations were quite a secondary consideration with him, and to my extreme satisfaction bathing was omitted on this occasion. My apparent objection to cleanliness will easily be understood when it is known that all the new arrivals, no matter how many, are plumped one after the other into the same water; and as many of them come in with all kinds of personal companions, a bath under these circumstances is hardly a thing to be desired.

The dragoon and Bob had fallen out over something or the other, and I could hear the latter grumbling and cursing at him; but the dragoon, being a determined kind of fellow, kept nagging away in return, until Old Bob poured forth such a sudden flood of vituperative abuse, that the young fellow was fairly frightened into silence. Bob's feelings were, I expect, considerably relieved by this outburst, for shortly after he came smiling into me in quite an amiable frame of mind.

"Well, how have you got on?" he demanded.

"Well, I have got a pair of shoes; they are nothing like a fit, but I suppose they must do, and if I can have a pair of laces I can, at all events, keep them on my feet."

"We ain't got any laces now, we are run right out of them, but we shall have some more down sooner or later, I suppose; but in the meantime I'll let you have a piece of string, and when the tailor has a little spare time I'll get him to make a pair of cloth inside soles for you, and that will fill up the shoes and keep your feet warm too."

The old chap was as good as his word, for a few nights later he brought me the inside soles in question, and a great comfort I found them, confined as one was in a cell floored with bare slates.

"Now, are your own clothes all ready to be packed up?" asked Bob.

"Yes, quite."

"Well, then, we'll just go over the list they have sent down from Z—— and see that the things are correct, and then you pack 'em up, and we'll seal the portmanteau and stow it away. The way some of these coves goes on that comes here," he continued, evidently referring to the dragoon, "is enough to drive a man mad. Why, you'd think they had a thousand a year; but I generally manages to teach 'em manners."

I thought to myself that if the address I had so lately heard him deliver was a specimen of the way he taught, I should not be much inclined to recommend his system. Whatever he may have been to others, however, "Old Bob" was exceedingly good-natured to me that night, so I must not be too hard upon his little weaknesses.

As soon as we had gone carefully over my clothes, with the Z—— list, and found everything correct, I bundled them all into the portmanteau, and Old Bob marched it off to the clothing store-room, assuring me as he departed that the place was kept thoroughly aired, and my things would come out at the end of the twelve months just as good as they were now.

A little later on, Bob bustled in to me again, and, after placing a large mess-tin full of tea and a huge piece of cake on the cell shelf, turned towards me, and after sundry winks, nods, and various expressive jerkings of his thumb over his shoulder towards the tea, hurried out again.

I was intensely amused at his exit, for I, feeling naturally very grateful to him, commenced to put my gratitude into words, but I no sooner began to speak than he put up his hands in horror, with a most impressive "hush-sh-sh," muttered, "Only going to forget them here by accident; swallow them up as quick as you can," and darted out of the door.

About seven o'clock the doctor arrived, and commenced his examination of the new arrivals. According to the regulations he was supposed to carefully examine every man before certifying him fit for first class hard labour; but as a matter of fact, the examination consisted of Old Bob's asking the men when they arrived whether they had anything the matter with them (and he did not always go through this form even), and if the answer was in the negative filling in their door-cards with "fit for first class labour," and giving them to the doctor to sign when he arrived. Even this ceremony was occasionally omitted, and I have known six and eight men in the prison at one time whose door-cards had all been signed with the doctor's initials by Old Bob himself, and the old fellow was foolish enough to boast to some of the other warders of how well he could imitate the doctor's signature. The consequence was that all kinds of scandalous cases were continually occurring—men who were subject to fits, and in a weak and sickly condition, were certified as fit for first class labour, and used to faint and fall from the wheel, doing themselves serious injury. There were two cases of this kind in quick succession on one occasion, and had the governor been anything of a sharp fellow he must have smelt a rat. The first was the case of a man who was sentenced to fourteen days' hard labour for begging. He was one of the most eccentric-looking men I ever saw. He had a long, thin, hatchet-shaped face, with a queer, plaintive, appealing look in his light, greenish-grey eyes, and a complexion of that unpleasant, underdone-meat colour, set off by pale, flaxen-coloured hair. His cheeks and upper lip were clean-shaved, but a Disraeli tuft on the underlip added to the curious *tout-ensemble* of this extraordinary-looking being. He was about six feet three inches in height, was a sawyer by trade and had been a preacher, was quite gone in the upper story, and subject to epileptic fits. He was, nevertheless, certified fit for first class labour and duly sent to work at the wheel.

The second day of this work brought on a fit, and some of the warders took the matter up and told Old Bob that he ought to take the doctor to examine the man again. This was done on the following day, and the doctor immediately exempted the man from hard labour. But it might have been too late, for a couple of days' wheel work was quite enough to have cost the fellow his life, and had any proper examination of him been made when he arrived the doctor could not have failed to see that the man was an idiot and in bad health.

The second case was that of a man sent in for four months' hard labour for deserting the militia. The second day he was on the wheel he had a fit, and came down a fearful crash on the slate flooring, and it was a perfect marvel to every one that he did not kill himself. He had been subject to fits, but no questions were asked him on admission, and this was the result. He was afterwards exempted from wheel labour; but his case was an extremely hard one, for the close confinement and want of proper food brought on a succession of these fits, and the man became so bad that an order was issued forbidding his attendance at chapel, and yet, notwithstanding the state of his health, he was never allowed one single scrap of additional food. The man looked in the most wretched state, and whether he ever lived to get out I do not know, for my sentence expired before he completed his.

These are only two cases out of many; but I mention these particularly because the men came under my own actual observation, and I most carefully inquired into both cases. Previously to this there had been a still more serious affair.

A man complained that he was subject to heart complaint; but the doctor and Old Bob got it into their heads that he was shamming, and the former certified him fit for first class labour.

It was very hot summer weather; the man was placed upon the wheel, and used to puff and blow and exhibit signs of intense distress while at work; but this was looked upon as a dodge, and no notice was taken of it, and the man continued at wheel work.

A few nights later the warder, going round to lock up the cell-doors at bedtime, heard a strange gurgling noise in this man's cell, and looking in, saw him stretched upon his bed gasping for breath. He sent for the chief warder, and drew his attention to the man's state; but the chief opined that the fellow was still shamming, and advised him " to give it up, as it wouldn't go down there."

As the chief warder uttered these words, the noise suddenly ceased, and the glazed eye, and curious dull leaden colour that spread over the man's face told its own tale. The chief warder would not, or could not, believe that the man was actually dead, and sent off post-haste for the doctor; but all the doctors in the world would have been of no avail, the end had come.

There was the usual inquest on the body, and the doctor stated the man had died from heart complaint, and the verdict was of course " Death from natural causes."

It is, perhaps, needless to say that all the true facts of the case were carefully suppressed; but worst of all, such a lesson even as this produced no permanent result, for not long afterwards another case of the same kind occurred.

The regulations for the doctor's examination of men before their discharge from the prison were equally disregarded, and the following case, one of the many that came under my immediate notice, is a fair example of what this examination consisted of.

The man was a naval prisoner in corridor D, and as Old Bob, followed by the doctor, came into the corridor from the receiving-ward, he walked forward to the man's cell (leaving the doctor at the foot of the staircase leading up to C corridor), opened the door about a foot, and shouted out, "You are all right and able to go out," slammed-to the door without waiting for any answer, and hurried up the staircase after the doctor.

I have particularly mentioned this man's being a naval prisoner because a special order had been sent down from the Admiralty requiring the doctor to be specially careful in his examination of naval men before their discharge. This order was made in consequence of one of the blue-jackets belonging to the flagship of the neighbouring port falling down dead as he was being escorted back to his ship after undergoing a short term of imprisonment.

The man in question had repeatedly complained to the doctor about his heart being bad and of his not feeling well, but no notice was taken of his grumblings (as they were called). He was kept at hard labour, and death from heart complaint was the natural result.

Meantime, the doctor has been running his eye over the other prisoners, and after a very cursory examination, judging from the short time it took, was shown into my cell by Old Bob.

The doctor had evidently dined, and I fancied a slight unsteadiness of gait was perceptible as he entered the cell.

"Well, how are you getting on?" he asked.

"I am not very well, thank you," I answered.

"Oh—ah! to be sure—to be sure! Well, I shall be able to exempt you from first class hard labour, as the state of your heart and chest preclude your being engaged in hard bodily labour. Just open your waistcoat," he continued, "and let me sound your chest again, so as to be quite satisfied."

I accordingly unbuttoned my things, though it struck me as rather an unnecessary proceeding, as the Z—— medical papers would show what the state of my health was. After sundry ineffectual attempts, he succeeded in applying his ear to the stethoscope, and after a moment's attention, followed by a heavy lurch forward, pulled himself up straight, saying,—

"Just so; to be sure. I shall exempt you from first class labour, and give directions that you are not to be tasked. By the way," he continued, "did they exempt you from first class labour at Z——?"

"Why, certainly, sir," I replied. "Didn't you see from my medical papers that I had been exempted from hard labour and ordered my bed, and milk and white bread?"

I could see from his face that he had never looked at my medical papers at all; but he said, "To be sure—to be sure. Well, you must try and get along as well as you can." And with this parting injunction he pulled himself together and shambled off.

About half-past seven Bob came and unlocked my door and told me to follow him, as I was now going to be taken up to my cell in the main prison.

I followed him out of the door, and found the dragoon awaiting my arrival, and, side by side, we marched along down the receiving-ward, through the iron doors, out into the D corridor, halting for a moment at the foot of the staircase until Bob's shout of "Prisoners coming up," brought Johns to the head of the steps, when, receiving the word to advance, I followed the dragoon up the steps into corridor C, where Johns took us in charge, and after showing me into cell No. 22, locked the door, and went off with the dragoon to some other part of the prison.

I looked round my narrow quarters, and could not repress an almost involuntary shudder as I thought of the twelve weary months that had to be passed in this hideous whitewashed receptacle.

A plank boarding, some six feet long by two feet and a half wide, raised about six inches from the ground by wooden trestles, was laying sideways against the wall, and brought home to my mind the unpleasant fact that the doctor had not after all made any order about my bed, and that I should be obliged to pass the night as best I could on this plank abomination.

Shortly after eight o'clock Johns came round to my cell to ask whether I had read and understood the rules and regulations; so I took the opportunity of asking him whether there was any special order as to what part of the cell the plank bed was to be placed in, and he informed me that I might put it where I pleased; but he advised me to place it in the right-hand corner, as that was out of the draught and handy to the hot-air entrance.

The bell for going to bed rang shortly after this, and I set to work to try and make the best bed I could with the sheets and blankets, retaining one blanket and the quilt as bed-clothes, and making the best mattress I could out of the rest.

There was a round wooden ledge at one end of the plank to do duty as a bolster, the

Government pillow, stuffed with cocoa-nut fibre, and about the size of a pincushion, being placed on this somewhat slippery shelf, and one's head hung out to dry, as it were, on this elegant superstructure. All attempts at sleep were unavailing, and I do not think I closed my eyes the whole night, and long before morning I was as sore all over as if I had been beaten with a good thick stick. I have been assured that it is only for the first night or two that it is uncomfortable, and that afterwards men can sleep as well on a plank as in a feather bed. I am thankful to say that I had no opportunity of proving the truth or falsehood of this statement, but feel morally certain that whatever other men might say I should never have got accustomed to this fiendish invention.

The county regulation about plank beds was an excellent one—only men who had been previously convicted were obliged to sleep on a plank for the first twenty-eight days. A man in prison for the first time getting his bed at once. There were several other regulations under the county granting slight privileges to first offenders, which were denied to the habitual criminal. Library-books, for instance, were allowed to the former at once, but the habitual had to earn them by steady good conduct for three months.

These admirable arrangements, admirable because they made prison thoroughly disagreeable to the persistent evil doer, were abolished by the Government, why or wherefore it is difficult to conceive, as they were some of the few sensible reforms introduced by the county authorities.

Gladly I hailed the sound of the rising-bell, as the warder marched along the corridor with it at five minutes past six, and with eager haste obeyed its summons, tumbling out of my so-called bed with an alacrity that would have delighted the strictest martinet had he been in ignorance of the cause of my prompt obedience. As soon as the bell ceases the warders go round their respective wards unlocking the cell-doors (which, I think I have explained, are always double-locked at night), and, at the same time, open the trap-doors, to pass in the various tools the men require for their day's work, and to make certain that the prisoners are out of bed. By the time the warder came round to my door I was half-dressed, for I found any attempt at more than smoothing myself over with the wet corner of my towel quite out of the question in the Government washing basin.

When the warder peeped in at my trap-door I took the opportunity of requesting him to be good enough to explain to me what I was supposed to do to my cell; whether it had to be washed over, or what had to be done to it, as there were no directions in the rules.

He told me in reply that he would come and give me any information I required as soon as he had finished unlocking the cell-doors.

I had just completed my toilette when my door was opened, and the warder entered. I looked at him with a good deal of natural curiosity, for I knew he was the warder of the corridor, and consequently upon him, in a great measure, it would depend whether my twelve months' sojourn was made bearable or unbearable.

The power of a corridor warder over the men in his ward is practically unlimited, and a bad-tempered, unscrupulous blackguard can easily make his portion of the prison a perfect hell upon earth. All the complaints or requests made by prisoners to the higher authorities are, as a matter of fact, decided by the warder, as a prisoner has orders to inform his corridor officer of any application he may intend making to the governor, before mentioning the matter to the latter, and, of course, if the warder tells the man that it is useless or unnecessary to make the request, the prisoner naturally holds his tongue.

If any particularly obstinate prisoner still persists in applying to the governor or inspector the result would be practically the same, as they would immediately ask the warder whether he knew of the matter, and if he replied in the negative the man would get reprimanded for not laying the matter in the first place before him. This was, at all events, the invariable rule at the Xshire Prison, and any application to the governor met with the stereotyped reply, " Oh, well, I'll see about it."

The seeing about it consisted of his consulting the chief warder and the corridor officer, and giving the prisoner the result of their advice on the following morning.

With easily understood eagerness I carefully scrutinized the features of the warder as he stood in the doorway for a second or two, quietly going through the same process with me. He was a tall, slight man, with good straight features, and considerable character and firmness about the chin, while the clear, calm, steadfast blue eye, gave one instinctively a feeling of trust and confidence in the man. With a large and varied experience of men and manners, gained in many parts of the world, I was accustomed to form a quick and generally pretty accurate idea of a person's character and disposition, and the result of my inspection was thoroughly favourable to the object of it. I had already been privately informed that Duke—this was his name—was the kindest-hearted and most straightforward warder employed inside the prison, and, looking at the man, I immediately felt that my informant was pretty well right, and after-experience fully bore out the information. He was deservedly popular amongst the prisoners, for he never deceived or worried them, and, though he kept strict discipline in his corridor, he was equally strict to all, and did not take dislikes to certain men, and then be perpetually reporting them, as some of the other warders were inclined to do. He was the only one of the warders that I never heard a word said against by any prisoner all the time I was in the prison, and this spoke volumes as to the sterling worth of his character, for I have known him frequently report men, and get them severely punished, but, as they always owned, if Duke reported them it was for some thoroughly good reason, and they deserved whatever punishment they got.

Rugby, the warder of B corridor, although a fine, venerable old fellow to look at, was inclined to indulge in little sneaky, underhand tricks, and would fidget and fuss over small trifling mistakes made by prisoners, till he nearly worried their lives out. He was a shifty, uncertain-tempered man, too, and inclined to make favourites of particular prisoners, though I am bound to say that he was consistently civil to me on the few occasions that I had anything to do with him.

Johns—who had at this time the A ward—I have already given a sketch of, and must certainly own that he was the most dissatisfied man I ever met with. He was in the habit of taking dislikes to certain men, and when he did would lead them a pretty dance; but I am bound to confess that, as a rule, it was the idle, troublesome fellows that he selected to worry.

Old Bob, who, amongst his other multitudinous duties, had the charge of D corridor, was a rough old dog, but as long as a man gave him no trouble, and asked for nothing, he would treat him pretty decently. He was certainly devoid of all ordinary feelings of humanity or kindness, and this, I presume, was one of the reasons why he was appointed to, and continued to hold, the post of hospital warder; and all the very small quantity of talent he possessed was employed in ministering to his own personal comforts, or devising some means of stealing a march upon his brother warders. He was a very close old chap, and it was usually extremely difficult to get any information out of him, unless you could come across him when he had had a few glasses of whisky; then he would talk nineteen to the dozen, and pretty revelations he used to let slip. The best time to get information out of Old Bob was on his return from a prisoner's funeral, and as hospital warder it was his duty to accompany to the grave the bodies of all men who died while undergoing imprisonment. This being looked upon as a special duty, he received half-a-crown from Government on each occasion; and, in addition to this, the undertaker always stood treat—as a sort of percentage on the job, I presume—and the consequence was that Old Bob invariably returned in a most loquacious and comical mood. Now was the time to hear him expatiate on the idiocy of the new Government regulations, and the inadequate manner in which the governor carried on the discipline of the prison. He used to tell me, with much bad language, and many regrets, that he had more writing to do now in a day than he had in a month under the county, and that it took up more than one man's time to fill in and sign the numerous forms that daily passed through his hands in his varied capacity as receiving, hospital, and corridor warder. There was a good deal of truth in this; but as Old Bob always had two cleaners, and took particular care that one of them should be a good writer, he had no such very great cause for complaint, as he invariably made the cleaner fill in the forms, he himself only signing them when completed.

But we must return to Duke, whom we have left standing at my cell-door all this time. After quietly looking me over for a few seconds, he advanced into the cell, and asked me what I wanted to know.

"Has my cell got to be washed out now?" I asked, "or what has to be done? I know nothing about washing and scrubbing, but if you will tell me exactly what is required I will do the best I can."

"It doesn't matter about washing your cell out every morning," he replied; "all that you have to see is that it is clean and neat; but if you are careful, and don't make it in a mess, twice a week will be quite sufficient. Be careful, however," he continued, "that you sweep it over every morning, and brush the dust up into the right-hand corner, and then my cleaner will take it away when he goes round with me after breakfast. Just give me your brush a moment, and I will show you what I mean."

"Can you tell me what work I shall have to do?" I asked.

"No, I don't know exactly," he replied; "Mr. Johns sees to all that; but you won't have to do very much, as I see the doctor has exempted you from first class labour. The governor goes round every morning after breakfast to inspect the men and their cells, so see that everything is in its place at that time: and be sure you have your stock on, and your cap off, as the governor is very particular on these points."

I afterwards discovered that this cap and stock question was a regular mania with the governor, and provided a man carefully carried this order out it did not matter what state his cell was in. So well was this known that it had become the subject of the following doggerel verse, which was repeated to each newcomer as one of the unpublished regulations to be strictly observed :—

> " Your cell may be dirty, and ragged your suit,
> Just stand to attention and salute ;
> Then if your stock you don, and your cap you doff,
> The Governor 'll easily let you off."

Meantime Duke had been brushing away at my cell, and now handing me the brush, told me to go on as I had seen him doing.

"That's right," said Duke approvingly, "you'll soon manage right enough; and when all the dust is swept up, take your floor cloth and just mop up any splashes of wet you may have made on the floor while washing. Are you well?" he continued, after looking fixedly at me for a minute or two.

"No," I replied; "I am not in good health."

"Oh, very well, I'll move you over to the other side of the corridor; it's the sunny side, and as I happen to have a vacant cell there you'll find it warmer and more cheerful than this."

I thanked him warmly, and he then left, for the bell was ringing for the men to go out and do their hour on the treadwheel before breakfast, and Duke had to stand at the top of the staircase leading into D corridor in order to prevent any attempt at talking as the men passed along. I set to work to get my cell put to rights, rolled up my bedding into a neat bundle, and placed it on the top shelf, then laid the plank sideways against the left-hand wall, passing it behind the table so as to prevent any possibility of its falling down, and after returning my basin, towel, combs, &c., to their proper places on the lower shelf, sat down to await my breakfast. During the course of the morning Duke moved me over to the opposite side of the corridor, and I found the cell, as he said, far brighter and warmer; and here I was located till the expiration of my sentence. It looked horribly bare and miserable at first, but I soon became quite accustomed to it, and used to imagine that it appeared more comfortable than any other cell in the corridor. .It is astonishing how living in a cell habituates you to it. I well remember on one occasion, when I had to move out of my cell for a day on account of the walls requiring re-whitewashing, and take up my abode for the time being in a cell on the opposite side, how hideously bare and uncomfortable I thought it looked after mine, although as a matter of fact it contained exactly the same amount of furniture. I was perfectly miserable until I got back to my own quarters. After seeing me safely installed, Duke advised me to try and get some kind of work to do, as otherwise I should feel the time hang so dreadfully heavily on my hands, and promised to send Johns down to me with some kind of light employment. A little later Johns entered my cell, and after a few preliminary grumbles, produced a large bunch of cocoa-nut fibre cord. Undoing the bundle, he threw four or five handfuls on the floor, and I then saw that they were short ends of fibre cord about half the thickness of my little finger, and varying in length from one or two inches to five or six.

"You want something to do, do you?" growled Johns. "Well, this is pretty easy kind of work; you have only got to pick the strands up one by one, and to twist them about until you have completely unravelled them. You have no call to hurry yourself, as the doctor has ordered you not to be tasked."

On his departure I set to work, and soon got into the knack of untwisting the fibre. It has to be carefully done, as it is used to stuff doormats with, and if the fibre is not thoroughly pulled apart, the mat-maker has endless trouble with it. The labour was purely mechanical, still it served for a day or two to occupy my attention and take my mind from the bitter, burning, regretful thoughts that crowded into my aching brain as I sat day after day involuntarily and unwillingly reviewing the past.

Unbidden and unwished for, the pale spectres of the past would come trooping into the lonely cell, and the life that might have been lay stretched before my eyes with an intensity of plainness that was well-nigh maddening. I have often wondered since how I managed to retain my senses, and if it had not been for the great kindness of the chaplain, who visited me almost daily at this time, I should have gone out of my mind without a doubt. Why Government cannot allow men convicted for the first time the use of library-books at once, instead of making them go without for the first eight weeks of their sentence, I cannot make out. It is a most useless and unnecessary barbarity, for without physically punishing a man it in many cases weakens him mentally, and sows the seeds of future madness.

The days now dragged along with hideous slowness, and to add to my other misfortunes, the doctor kept me on the regular diet, although I had come down from Z—— with my medical papers showing that the doctor there considered that I required extra diet. I do not believe the doctor here ever saw the medical papers—or if he did he did not take the trouble to read them—for on my applying to him to exempt me from sleeping on a plank bed, he at once asked me if they had exempted me at Z——. Now, if he had looked at the medical papers, he must have known whether this was the case or not, as it was all fully stated there. I assured him that they had given me my bed, and so he said, "To be sure, to be sure," and made an order for me to have my hammock. This was a slight improvement, although it was some time before I became accustomed to packing myself in this semi-circular abomination, but in course of time my backbone got properly crooked, I suppose, and I managed to sleep fairly well. It seems rather hard lines, though, that men imprisoned at Z—— should have a really comfortable bed to sleep in, while those whose little failings take place in the adjoining county have to put up with these hammocks. The Sundays at first seemed fearfully long; there was nothing on earth to do, and once afternoon chapel was over, one was shut up for five mortal hours ere the welcome bell at eight o'clock rang out permission to go to bed. One is allowed no exercise for the first twenty-eight days, so that weekdays and Sundays I was mewed up in my cell, with nothing whatever to look at but the four whitewashed walls. To make matters worse they were busy altering the chapel, cutting down all the old coffin-like boxes, and arranging it in open seats; so that I did not even obtain the change of scene and air that the daily quarter of an hour's chapel usually afforded. After about a fortnight it became unbearable, and I got hold of Johns one afternoon and asked him if I could not learn how to make a mat.

"Yes, if the governor will give you leave," was his reply; and the following morning I stopped the governor as he was going his rounds, and asked the question.

"Make mats!" he replied; "yes, certainly; but you cannot commence that until you have been here twenty-eight days."

"Oh, I thought as the doctor had certified me unfit for first class labour, I might begin at once, sir," I said.

He hummed and hawed a little, and then turning to the chief warder, asked him if this was so. The chief bit his lip, and seemed lost in thought for a minute or two, and finally said he believed I might begin at once according to the Government regulations.

Whether the chief made this reply from ignorance, or out of kindness to me, it is of course impossible for me to say; but as a matter of fact it was strictly contrary to the regulations to allow me to commence before the expiration of twenty-eight days. I was delighted at the success of my application, and that afternoon Johns brought me a mat-frame and the various other materials required, and proceeded to show me how to manufacture a door-mat. He took a lot of trouble to teach me properly, and though he would occasionally break out into fearful fits of grumbling, I soon got hold of the knack of the thing, and managed to turn out a very decent mat after a fortnight's practice. Mat-making is a thing that any fool could learn, but what I do not understand is how men manage to make mats at the pace they do. I spent about two months at this employment, and yet I could never manage to make a mat in less than two days. Now men who were certified fit for first class labour were required to make ten of these same mats in the week, and if they did not complete their task they were reported to the governor, and very soon found themselves on short commons. There was no method in the tasking, and the man convicted for the first time, and who knew no more of mat-making than he did of Greek, would be ordered to make exactly the same number of mats a week as the habitual criminal who, from being constantly in and out of prison, thoroughly understood the trade. The natural consequence was that some of the prisoners had to work like slaves, while the old hands, who really deserve to be made uncomfortable, got through their work with very little trouble, for they knew exactly what to do, and how to do it.

There is another thing that is very unfair to the prisoner in this tasking system, and that is his being obliged to work during the hours of rest allowed him at various times during the day by the Government regulations. When men are tasked their tools ought to be taken away from them during these appointed hours, and returned to them again when work time begins. In this way the authorities could easily find out, if they chose to take the trouble, those men who were really unable to perform their allotted task, either from want of skill or from physical weakness, and they could then reduce their weekly number of mats until they had time to master the trade.

Here let me call attention to a very great imposition practised on the prisoners at Xshire, and, I daresay, at other prisons. According to the Government regulations a prisoner is to be allowed half an hour in which to dress and do up his cell, and three-quarters of an hour for breakfast, an hour and a half for dinner, and half an hour for tea, making an aggregate of three hours and a quarter's rest during the day. This is not at all an extravagant amount, when you consider that a prisoner commences at six o'clock in the morning and has to go on working till eight o'clock at night.

A copy of these regulations is hung up in the main corridor of every prison, close to the warder's office; but there is no mention of them whatever in the rules issued to the prisoners, and the latter have no opportunity of seeing them in the corridor. The consequence is that there is not one prisoner in a hundred who knows that he is entitled to any rest at all; and at Xshire they used to gobble down their meals as fast as they could, and return at once to their work. Either a copy of these regulations ought to be placed in each man's cell, or the warder of each corridor ought to have strict orders to read them over to each new arrival in his ward.

At Z—— men were always told what time they had to themselves, and a bell for recommencing work used to ring after each meal, as soon as the allotted time had expired. This was doing things in a straightforward manner, and the Commissioners ought to see that the same thing was done in every prison.

Now that I had got some employment to interest me and to take up my attention the time began to pass a good deal quicker; but just at this time my health began to utterly break down, and to make matters worse I got an attack of dysentery. This last complaint was brought on by the gruel. I was quite unable to digest it, and had asked the doctor again and again if he would change it for me, but without avail. I became very ill, and must have been pretty bad, for several of the warders afterwards told me that they never expected I should have lived; yet I could not get the doctor to do anything but dose me with physic, which did not do me the slightest good, and must have cost the Government a considerable sum, for I had eight or nine different kinds of medicine in my cell at a time. I could not understand it at all, for although the poor old doctor was generally more or less screwed, I had managed to get hold of him once or twice when he was quite sober, and I knew he must know that I was in a very queer state, and in dire need of some kind of substantial nourishment. One fine day, however, the cat came out of the bag. I had the doctor down to see me, and after telling him how very weak I felt, asked him if he would place me on milk and white bread diet, as the doctor at Z—— had done. He told me he would consider the matter, and after promising to send me down some medicine "that would do me good," walked out of my cell with Old Bob at his heels. I have already stated, I think, that Bob, being hospital warder (unless he happened to be off duty), always went round with the doctor. Old Bob had no sooner shut my door than I heard the doctor say to him,—

"Bob, that man requires a change of diet; he is very ill."

"Oh, I shouldn't, sir," replied Old Bob; "he ain't lost much weight, and I shouldn't make any change yet."

"To be sure, to be sure," answered the doctor; "I won't make any alteration at present, but I must soon."

They now passed on down the corridor, and I was unable to hear the remainder of their conversation, but I did not get my milk and bread. I had, however, the satisfaction of knowing who it was that was preventing my getting the food I needed; though I could not at first make out what motive Old Bob could have, but a few inquiries soon brought this to light. I discovered that whenever any food outside the prison dietary was ordered for a prisoner, Old Bob had to see after it and bring it up to the prisoner; so if the doctor had ordered me milk it would have given Bob the trouble of coming up and down to me with it every morning and evening, and Bob would have sooner seen fifty prisoners die than have had to take that much trouble.

It is a great blot on the present system that the warder on whom the extra trouble falls should invariably go round with the surgeon. He naturally objects to having a prisoner moved up to the hospital, or placed on any special diet, and does his best to prevent the doctor doing anything for a man as long as he possibly can. It would be much better if each warder went round his own corridor with the surgeon; he would be far better able to judge whether a man was failing, for he has him under his daily observation, and his opinion would be of some use to the doctor. The warder could take down in writing the instructions of the doctor with respect to each prisoner, and then hand them over to the hospital warder to see them duly carried out. If the corridor warder was made responsible for any mistakes arising from these instructions not being immediately attended to, he would take precious good care that the hospital warder did his duty.

At Xshire they would not even carry out the present system in a proper manner, and the medical and hospital arrangements were simply disgraceful. The doctor came frequently to the prison, after having dined far too generously at home, and could then be induced to say anything that Old Bob told him. There was no secret about this; the prisoners, warders, and even the chaplain knew it, and it was not a state of things that ought to have been tolerated for a moment. He was an exceedingly clever man, so much so that the townspeople averred, if dangerously ill they would sooner have him drunk than any other doctor sober; and being in addition as jovial and good-hearted a fellow as ever stepped, nobody liked to say anything about him. He was so drunk one night that he fell down twice in trying to get up the staircase to B corridor, and on another occasion he left the key in the surgery door, and went off home; and if one of the warders had not luckily happened to see it, one of the prisoners employed in cleaning the passage might have slipped in and got enough poison to do for all hands.

Instead of making Old Bob stand to attention at the door of the cell and simply take down his instructions, the doctor used to allow him to lounge into the cell and cross-question the men; and in most cases it was Bob who did all the talking, while the doctor simply looked on and said occasionally, "To be sure, to be sure."

If a man was sent up to the hospital Old Bob had to go up and down stairs three or four times a day with the food for him, which of course entailed a considerable amount of extra trouble; so you may be quite sure he prevented a prisoner being moved from his cell as long as he possibly could. The consequence of this was that several men were kept down in their cells, on ordinary prison diet, until they were so far gone that moving them into hospital was an utterly useless farce. There were three most scandalous cases of this description that came under my own immediate notice during the twelve months I was at the prison, and I may as well briefly recapitulate them here, as it will prove beyond a doubt how much need of reform there is in the present system. No. 1 was the case of a marine named B———t, undergoing a sentence of six months' imprisonment for desertion. He was rather a delicate man, and the confinement and mat-making rapidly told upon his constitution, and his lungs became affected. There is a fine, powdery dust given off by cocoa-nut fibre that impregnates the air, covers the cell, and finds its way into your nose, ears, and throat, causing the greatest irritation to the latter, and most injurious to any one with weak lungs. B———t had the doctor to see him several times, but I presume Bob did the prescribing, as the man was never ordered any extra food, or excused any portion of his allotted task of mat-making. The man gradually went from bad to worse, till within three weeks of his discharge, when one morning the corridor warder went into his cell, as he happened to see the floor was in a great mess, and found that the man had been spitting blood all night, and the place was in a pretty state. The warder forthwith put B———t's name down on the sick list, and told the doctor the state in which he had found the man's cell. B———t was accordingly interviewed by the doctor and Bob, and the former told him he would send him some medicine, but certified him fit for duty, although he told the corridor warder that the man was very bad and had hardly any chance of recovery. The unfortunate man went on at his work for another week, and then completely broke down. The doctor's attention was again directed to him, and he now made an order that he was to do no more work, but gave him no extra food, and would not make an order for him to be moved into the hospital, as Old Bob said his sentence expired in another ten days, and it was not worth the trouble. The doctor seemed to take the same view, for he said "he did not know whether he would live to get out, and it was better to leave him alone."

B——t did live to go out, but was so bad when he left that his death was certain, and it was a mere question of time. Now whether the man's life might not have been saved if he had been placed in the hospital and properly fed is best known to the doctor, but I have no doubt on the matter myself.

In case No. 2 the man was also a marine, whom we will call Smith. He was transferred to us from another prison on the 5th September, and as soon as the doctor saw him, he declared it to be a hopeless case. Smith only had another month to serve before his sentence expired, but the doctor expressed serious doubts as to his living to go out. This is the state of health in which the man arrived, yet with only a month more to do, they had sent him from the other prison a railway journey of two hours and a half, with the knowledge that on arriving at Xshire station he would have a three miles' drive in a draughty omnibus ere he reached our prison, and yet knowing all this the doctor certified this man, dying of consumption, asthma, and half a dozen other complications, to be in a fit state of health to make this journey. Now, I do not like to say anything disagreeable about a man I know nothing about, but I must own that I think that doctor must have been either a great fool or a great scoundrel. Our doctor was, unfortunately, pretty nearly as bad as the other, for although he considered Smith's case such a very serious one, he never ordered him up to the hospital or made any difference in the diet for him, but just treated him as if he were in ordinary health. The doctor having made no order about the man he was obliged to get up and do his cell out, and sit about as best he could during the day, but in a very short time he became quite incapable of sitting up, and used to lie about on the slate flooring of the cell—a nice couch for a man in consumption. The doctor's attention was now called to him by the corridor warder, and an order was made for him to have his hammock to lie on of a day, and to have tea and white bread in lieu of gruel and brown. His bones were nearly through his skin and he was quite unable to eat coarse food, so this was not much good to him. He gradually went from bad to worse, but the doctor would not move him up to the hospital or order him any proper diet, and the whole of the upper end of the corridor was becoming most offensive, for the poor fellow was just rotting away, and the stench was fearful. It at last became so bad that the corridor warder interfered and told the doctor that the man must be moved out of the corridor, and although old Bob still maintained that it was "no use troubling," the other warder held out about it, and finally on the 22nd of September, Smith was taken up to the hospital, and a couple of other prisoners told off to look after him. He was now, however, sinking rapidly, so the doctor thought he might safely order him beef tea, brandy, and anything else he wished for, as he could not be long an expense; and his premises were quite correct, for on the 26th the man died. On the 27th the inquest was held, and the doctor explained to the jury how he had ordered the man tea and white bread, and sent him up to the hospital, and given him brandy, beef tea, &c., but he quite forgot to say that he left him in his cell until within four days of his death, and only ordered him nourishing food when he was actually dying. Whether the man ever would have recovered, even if properly treated, is, I should imagine, extremely doubtful; but whatever doubt there may be about that, there can be no doubt whatever that his death was considerably accelerated by the manner in which he was treated.

The third case was a still more scandalous one, and as it proves conclusively how useless the existing regulations are in protecting a prisoner from ill-treatment, I purpose giving a full and careful detail of it, and, in order to prevent any mistake or over-colouring, have taken the narrative almost verbatim from the diary I kept while in prison, and in which I entered, day by day, all particulars of this case as they occurred.

The prisoner, Thomas K——n, was also,

funnily enough, a marine, and was undergoing a sentence of two years' hard labour for threatening to murder his sergeant. He was a hot-tempered Irishman, but when let alone was a decent enough fellow, as far as I could judge from what I saw and heard about him. A broad-built, powerful-looking fellow of two-and-twenty, he ought to have stood his punishment well enough if only fairly treated. After K——n had been a short time at the prison he was employed at one of the looms to make cocoa-nut matting under the supervision of Johns. I have already stated what a surly, ill-tempered, disagreeable man Johns was (though it was more manner than anything else), and whether K——n's hot Irish blood rebelled at being bullied and growled at, or whether Johns took a dislike to him, I do not know, but they fell out over something or the other, and it is quite certain that Johns did not make the place a bed of roses for K——n. They were continually quarrelling about the work, K——n saying that Johns was overtasking him, and never satisfied no matter how hard he worked, and Johns declaring that K——n was an idle, insolent scoundrel. K——n finally complained to the governor saying that Johns was always reporting and getting him into trouble, although he was doing his best, and finished up with, "there's not a single other officer in the prison that I have had a word with, sir; they'll tell you that I have always obeyed orders, and done the best I could."

The governor declined to make any inquiries amongst the other warders as to the character he bore, and told him he must do more work and behave better. Things went on in the same way for another month or so, and then K——n complained to the visiting magistrates when they came round on their monthly visit. The chairman of the committee, who always listened patiently to any complaints that were made, and carefully inquired into them, heard K——n's story, discussed it with the other magistrates, and after examining Johns, and going over the whole matter, made an order that K——n should be no longer employed at the loom, but be given other work in his cell.

This is proof positive that K———n must have had just and reasonable grounds for his complaint, or the magistrates would never have made such an order as this. K———n was now employed in making mats in his own cell, still, however, under the supervision of Johns, who expressed the same dissatisfaction with his mat-making as he had previously done about his loom work. Once more K———n complained to the governor, and although the latter gave *him* no satisfaction, simply telling him that he must not be making complaints about the officers, he must have thought that there was something in it, for he sent for Johns and told him he was not to report K———n any more, unless he could call some other officer to prove that the complaint was correct. The governor also made an order that the chief warder was to see after K———n's mat-making instead of Johns.

To complain about a warder to the visiting magistrates and the governor was in itself a most dire offence to the warders, but to gain a tacit victory, as K———n undoubtedly had, was a state of things that could not be allowed, and the warders put their heads together and determined to make it hot for him. K———n was now beginning to complain of being ill, and to apply to the doctor for a little extra food, so the warders agreed amongst themselves that whoever went round with the doctor was to take good care that he did not give him anything extra, but whenever K———n applied they were to persuade the doctor that he was a lazy fellow trying to humbug him by shamming. They were perfectly successful in their scheme, for although K———n frequently applied to the doctor, the latter would never give him any extra food, and after three or four successive applications sent word to K———n by the corridor warder that he was not to ask for extra food any more, as he would not give it to him.

It was now December, and K———n had completed some ten months of his sentence, and it is a most significant fact, that he was the only man that had passed more than nine months in the prison who had not got extra diet of some kind. Early in January K———n again sent for the doctor, complaining that he was dreadfully weak and ill, and begged very hard for a little extra food, but without avail.

I happened one day to be out dusting in the corridor when the doctor came to go his rounds. He nodded to me as he passed along, and asked me how I was getting on, and made some cheery remarks about my time being nearly out (for he was always exceedingly kind to me in this way), and as he went on I heard old Bob say, "There are only two men on the report to-day, sir, No 36 and No. 10 (K———n); here we are at 36, sir." The doctor entered the cell, heard what the man wanted, and then went on to the warder's office at the end of the corridor. I followed along dusting away at the door numbers and locks and heard Bob say, "There's only K———n, No. 10, to see now, sir," and then he said a few words to him in a low tone, to which the doctor replied, "To be sure, to be sure; send him up here."

Bob shuffled down the corridor, unlocked K———n's door, and told him to go up to the head of the corridor if he wanted to see the doctor. K——n marched up the corridor, stood to attention in front of the doctor, and saluted.

"Well, K——n, what's the matter with you?" he asked.

"If you please, sir, I am very weak and ill; could you let me have a little change of food?"

"You are on the fourth class, arn't you?"

"Yes, sir," replied K——n, "but I cannot get on at all, sir."

"Well, I cannot make any alteration, but I'll send you some medicine."

And K——n, with another salute, marched back to his cell, and as he passed along there was a weary, hopeless look on the man's face that made my heart ache. Now the doctor refused his application without making any examination of the man whatever, and within six weeks the man was dead of consumption. It is absurd to suppose that he could have been in perfect health at this time. Johns and the chief warder now put their heads together and reported K——n for being idle and neglecting to complete his allotted weekly task. The chief backed this report up to the governor, who had

K——n up to his office, lectured him on his idleness, and sentenced him to fifteen days' bread and water, with solitary confinement. K———n begged the governor to let him off, declaring that he was so ill and weak that he could hardly walk up to the office, and really had been working as hard as he possibly could. He begged so hard that the governor finally made an order that the doctor was to see him and report whether he was in a fit state of health to undergo the punishment. That night the doctor examined him, and reported that the man was rather weak and ill, and on the following day the governor had K———n once more up to his office, and told him he would let him off this time, but he trusted that his forbearance on this occasion would render him more diligent in the future. The unfortunate fellow tried now to complete the task set him, with the result that the following week (the third week in January) he was seized with an attack of hemorrhage of the lungs, and was ordered by the doctor to keep his bed, and he at the same time made an order for him to have white bread for a fortnight, in lieu of brown. The poor fellow had had a bad cough for some time, but it now got fearfully bad; and I used to be awakened again and again during the night by the noise he made.

I was at this time employed by the corridor warder to go round every evening with him and light the gas in the different cells, so that I had an opportunity of seeing K———n every evening, and naturally made the best use of my opportunities. In a day or two K———n apparently got over this attack, or, I presume, the doctor thought he had, for he was certified fit for work again, and I myself saw him hard at work at his mats on the 27th or 28th of January. A couple of days' work in his present state of health very soon did for him, and on the 2nd of February he had to take to his bed again, and on the following day the doctor told Duke, the corridor warder, that the man was very ill, and he was afraid he would not recover. On the 4th of February K———n asked the doctor if he would let him have a little tea to slake the burning thirst with which he was troubled at night, and the doctor said " To be sure, certainly;" but being, as usual, three sheets in the wind, forgot all about the matter, and old Bob, not remembering it either, let the doctor go away without making out or signing the necessary order. Later on K——n applied to Duke to know if he could have the tea the doctor had promised him; and on Duke asking old Bob about it, the latter said, oh, he had forgotten about it, and wasn't going to be bothered; the fellow must do without it. Duke was storming away in the corridor about it like mad. I could overhear him saying to old Bob "that it was a shame, and that he supposed he should have to make the man some tea out of his own supply, but he didn't at all see why he was to have to pay for tea for a man because Bob was too lazy to see that the doctor wrote out the proper orders. Bob's reply was straight to the point, he declared " he didn't care a d—— what Duke did with his d—— tea, he wasn't going to trouble his head about the d—— fellow;" and away he bounced down the stairs. I afterwards made inquiries and learned that Duke did make K——n a pint of tea himself, and brought it to him, but I don't suppose there was another warder in the prison who would have done the same thing. The following day, February 5th, the doctor again promised K———n that he would let him have tea and white bread, but once more he forgot all about it, and old Bob let him go away without making any order, so unfortunate K———n was again left in the lurch. Whether old Bob purposely let the doctor go away without making the necessary order, or whether he really forgot it, I should not like to say, but the possibility of such a mistake arising once, let alone twice, would have been avoided if old Bob had been made to stand to attention at the door of the cell, like the hospital warder at Z———, and take down on a slate whatever the doctor ordered for a man, and then afterwards read the list out to the doctor in the surgery.

K———n could now eat nothing, and was evidently very bad indeed, yet the doctor would not send him up to the hospital, but kept him down in his cell. One of the consequences of this was that whenever the gas was lighted by any warder but Duke, K———n used to have to plump out on to the cold slate floor, take the candle as it was passed through the trap-door, light his gas, and then tumble into bed again; a nice arrangement for a man in his state of health.

I copy the following from my diary:—

On the 6th of February K———n had another desperate attack of hemorrhage of the lungs, and his cough is so distressing that it is disturbing everybody in the corridor. To-day the doctor said he was so bad that he thought he couldn't get over it, and Duke suggested that he should be sent up to the hospital, as it wouldn't do for him to be dying in his corridor; and after some discussion the doctor made an order for his being moved to-morrow, but never made any order for any extra food or stimulants to try and keep up the man's strength.

To-day (Saturday, February 7th) K———n is to be moved up into hospital, and during the morning the chief came into the corridor and held a long consultation with Duke as to what two prisoners are to be selected to look after K———n while he is in hospital.

"We must be careful whom we select," said the chief, "and on no account send any naval men, or they will be spreading all sorts of stories when they go out."

Then I heard Duke suggest that I should be sent as one, but the chief said, "Good gracious! on no account, on no account."

The chief finally settled upon a decent kind of man, a pianoforte tuner by trade, who was undergoing a sentence of imprisonment only, and a little labouring man, who was as deaf as a post. The idea of selecting a man who was stone deaf for a nurse was peculiarly brilliant, but the fact was it was such a scandalous case they were afraid of letting anybody more than they could possibly help know anything about it. During the afternoon they proceeded to move K——n up to the hospital, and as I was out dusting in the corridor, I carefully inspected the whole affair. About four o'clock Podgers, who was the warder in charge of the removal, went to K——n's cell with 8 D and 6 B, the two men selected as nurses, and ordered the unfortunate man to get out of bed, and get his clothes on, and then, as best he could, with one of the men on one side, and the other on the other, he had to walk up to the hospital. This was a pretty way to move a dying man. Fancy taking a man out of his bed, making him dress, and then conducting him down the corridor, with a door leading out into the open air thrown wide open at the further end, then along a draughty passage, and finally up a flight of stairs to the hospital. Still that's the way they did things here. Even now that he is in hospital the doctor does not allow him any extra diet, with the exception of the white bread.

From the 7th to the 14th K——n gradually got worse, and the doctor told the governor that it was impossible for him to recover, and the best thing to do was to release him and send him to his friends. This was a regular dodge.; as soon as a man's case was hopeless they got an order for his release from the Home Secretary and sent him home, so that his family might have the expense of burying him. In the present case, however, it would not do, as poor K——n was an orphan, and had neither kith nor kin, so they had to keep him whether they liked it or not.

On Saturday, the 14th February, they thought he was dying, and the priest (K———n was a Roman Catholic) came to administer extreme unction, but found K———n quite unconscious. Now that it was too late the doctor made an order that K———n was to have anything he fancied, and under the influence of beef-tea and other things he rallied a little on Sunday, though he was still light-headed at times, for on Duke going up to see how he was on Sunday afternoon, and asking him how he was, K———n imagined he was old Bob, but on Duke's again speaking to him and saying, "Why, don't you know me? I am not Bob," K———n replied, "Of course I do, you are Mr. Duke, you saved my life by getting me sent up here when the doctor wouldn't take any notice of what I said."

The sort of feeling there was about K———n amongst the warders will be best shown by relating what occurred on the Saturday afternoon.

I was walking along the corridor behind Duke, in order to get the candles, and start lighting the gas, when Humphrey, the miller warder, came up to Duke and said,—

"So No. 10's dying, is he? that's a good job; we'll teach them to report officers."

On Monday, the 16th, K——n was apparently better, the extra diet seeming to have put some life into him, and when the doctor saw him he made an order that he was to have a couple of eggs beaten up in half a tumbler of brandy every day to try and keep up his strength, the mixture to be administered in small quantities at various times during the day. There is a strict order that wines, spirits, or indeed any extra delicacies ordered by the doctor, are not to be left in the hospital room, for the prisoners who are acting as nurses to give to the sick man, but must be handed to him by the hospital warder and eaten or drunk, as the case may be, in the presence of the warder. This being the case, you may be quite sure old Bob did not take the trouble to go up to the hospital two or three times a day to administer these kind of things, but used to make one journey do.

On Monday evening K——n was decidedly

better, and ate, for a sick man, a hearty tea. He had just finished the meal, when old Bob, who was going off duty at six o'clock, came bustling up with a tumbler full of brandy and eggs, and handing it to K———n said,—

"Now, then, swallow this; look sharp."

K———n did as he was ordered, and then gasping for breath said,—

"Why, it's spirits."

You can imagine the kind of effect this was likely to have upon a man who had not tasted any intoxicating liquor for twelve months, and was at the time worn out with disease. It stupefied him for a bit, and then later on in the night brought on such a fit of raving delirium, that it required the united strength of both his nurses to keep him in his bed. A pretty time they had with him all night, but towards morning he sank into a kind of stupor, from which he never rallied, and died at 4.30 on Wednesday afternoon, February 18th.

I have been very particular with the dates in this case, because they show more than anything else how the man was neglected until all hopes of saving his life were past. The chaplain's comment on K——n's death was pretty significant.

"Ah, they were not long doing for him. I thought it was not all temper."

While K——n's body was awaiting the inquest, a doctor was sent down from the Home Office to examine the prison, and he, I fancy, was rather surprised that K——n had not been sooner sent to the hospital, for some little time after the Xshire doctor got a letter from the prison commissioners, asking why he had not sent K——n up to hospital sooner. What excuse he made I do not know, but there the matter ended. A prisoner's chance of getting over a serious illness was pretty small, when one calmly considers the odds against him—a careless doctor (under certain circumstances), a brutal, unscrupulous hospital warder, and a couple of ignorant labourers to act as nurses.

It may perhaps be thought that I have exaggerated this account, but it is not the case, I have, on the contrary, been most careful to keep well within bounds, and am prepared, if necessary, to substantiate from the lips of the officials themselves every word that I have stated above.

The hospital regulations, drawn up by the authorities, are faulty enough in themselves, but when they are not even properly carried out, the unfortunate prisoner has a very poor chance. The present system of appointing prisoners to act as nurses is utterly bad, and the sooner the authorities make some alteration the better. There ought to be a warder appointed whose sole duty it should be to attend upon the doctor, give out medicines, and look after any man that was moved up into hospital. By looking after a man I mean that he should be with the sick man day and night; let him have his bed in the hospital and give him a prisoner to do the washing and rough work. He ought, of course, to have some knowledge of sickness and disease, and there might be some difficulty in obtaining the man I have suggested, but difficulty ought not to be allowed to stand in the way, for when prisoners are dangerously ill they ought to be treated like men, and not like brutes. There is a special hospital diet, drawn up by the authorities, which I give below, and I am morally certain that a prisoner is supposed to be placed on this diet as soon as he is ordered into hospital by the doctor. This was never done at X-shire, but the prisoner was kept on his ordinary diet until the doctor chose to make a special order.

HOSPITAL DIETARY.

L.P.
M. 11.

MEN AND WOMEN.

PER DAY.

Diets.	Bread.	Cooked Mutton (without Bone).	Cooked Fresh Fish.	Potatoes.	Rice Pudding.	Arrowroot (made with milk).	Tea.	Milk, additional to that in Arrowroot.
	ounces.	ounces.	ounces.	ounces.	ounces.	ounces.	ounces.	ounces.
Ordinary	16	5	...	8	8	...	30	...
Extra . .	20	6	...	8	8	...	30	...
Fish . .	16	...	10	8	...	...	30	...
Low . .	8	...	...	...	...	20	15	20

The following articles may be ordered as extras or substitutes, in the quantities deemed necessary by the medical officer :—

Ale.   Beef Tea.
Bacon.   Biscuits.

Butter.
Cake.
Cocoa.
Corn Flour.
Eggs.
Fruit.
Greens (or other vegetables in lieu of Potatoes).
Ice.
Jam.
Jelly.
Lemonade (see below).
Milk.
Porter.
Poultry.
Rice (ground).
Sago.
Spirits.
Stout.
Sugar.
Waters (Mineral).
Wine.

INSTRUCTIONS.

Rice Pudding . .	2 ounces rice; 1 pint milk; 1 ounce sugar; 1 egg and nutmeg, to produce 20 ounces.
Arrowroot . .	1 ounce arrowroot; 1 pint milk; 1 ounce sugar, to produce 1 pint
Beef Tea . .	16 ounces of the lean parts of the neck of the ox to 1 pint of water.
Tea	$\frac{1}{8}$ ounce tea; $\frac{3}{4}$ ounce sugar; 2 ounces milk; and water to make up $\frac{3}{4}$ pint.
Cocoa . . .	$\frac{3}{4}$ ounce flaked or admiralty cocoa to 1 pint water, sweetened with $\frac{3}{4}$ ounce molasses or sugar, for flaked cocoa, and $\frac{1}{2}$ ounce molasses or sugar for admiralty cocoa.
Lemonade . .	$\frac{1}{4}$ ounce cream of tar; $\frac{1}{2}$ lemon (sliced), 2 ounces of loaf sugar, water, 1$\frac{1}{2}$ pints. The water to be added hot to the other ingredients, and the whole to be allowed to stand till cold; then strain.
Mutton . . .	To be roast or baked on 4 days in the week, and boiled on 3 days. On the days on which the mutton is boiled the meat liquor to be thickened with $\frac{1}{4}$ ounce flour, and flavoured with $\frac{1}{4}$ ounce onions per diet.
(3.)	Printed at H.M. Convict Prison, Millbank. 9—7.

From the above dietary the conclusion will be drawn, I think—having regard to the word *ordinary* as the first on the table—that men are supposed to be placed on this first-mentioned diet as soon as they are sent into hospital; and surely this ought to be the case, for if a man is so ill as to necessitate his being sent to the infirmary he must, *a fortiori*, need some better food than the ordinary prison diet.

From the list of extras it will be seen that there is practically no limit to the doctor's power of ordering any kind of nourishing food that an invalid can possibly need, and that if a prisoner does not get all he requires it is the fault of the medical officer, not of the authorities, though, of course, the latter are to a certain extent to blame for not seeing that their rules and regulations are properly carried out.

At Xshire the general arrangements for the hospital were just as bad as they could be. The accommodation, although pretty fair as far as it went, was far too limited, and the ventilating and sanitary arrangements simply abominable. There were no special food utensils set apart for use in the hospital, and the consequence was that old Bob had to take the food up in the ordinary prison mess-tins; and these tins would be used by the sick men in hospital one day and in the prison the next. Supposing any contagious sickness broke out, what a quick and easy method this would be for spreading the infection.

The argument used in prisons, that if they made the hospital comfortable prisoners would always be shamming ill in order to get sent there, is not, or at all events ought not to be, a sound one, for a competent medical man should be able to discover in a very short time whether a man is really ill or not. They say that if a man takes pills made of common soap they will in a short time so affect him that he will appear to be in the last stage of atrophy, and that it is impossible for a doctor to tell whether he is really suffering from atrophy or only undergoing a course of soap.

At Xshire the warders told me that several men had obtained their release by taking these pills, before it was discovered that soap did have this effect upon men, but now that it is a known fact one would think that a medical man would have no difficulty in discovering it.

They had a course of treatment at Xshire for men whom they suspected to be shamming that was very grand in its conception, but was likely to result in very disastrous consequences if the man upon whom they were experimentalizing happened to be really ill. A case of this kind came under my observation whilst there, and I may as well give a slight sketch of it here. The prisoner was a boy in the royal navy, aged fifteen, and sentenced to three months' hard labour. After being a week or two at the prison he complained of being ill, and was found one day lying insensible on the floor of his cell. The doctor was sent for, and the boy moved into the hospital. A couple of other prisoners were sent up to nurse him, and the doctor attended him daily, but could not make out what was the matter with the boy. There happened to be an old man ill in hospital at the same time, so they kept the boy up in the hospital whilst the doctor tried to discover what was the matter with him.

The hospital windows looked out upon the warders' gardens, and one night old Bob happened to go up there to get some vegetables after he had locked up the hospital for the night. The men, thinking old Bob safely away at his quarters, were chattering away like so many magpies, and Bob, as he passed under the windows, heard the sound of loud talking and laughing. He at once returned to the prison and gently let himself in, took off his boots at the foot of the staircase leading up to the hospital, crept quietly up the stairs, applied his eye to the spy-hole of the door, and took a general survey of the whole scene. The nurse was standing with his back to the fire, the boy was sitting up in bed with the pillow at his back, while the old man was sitting on the edge of his bed swinging his antiquated heels to and fro, and the whole party were talking away as hard as they could go. Bob, the deep old file, quietly walked down stairs again, pulled on his boots, and then came pounding up the staircase, making as much noise as he could, unlocked the door, and marched in. The inmates were all in bed, and apparently sound asleep. Shaking with anger, Bob stepped up to the old man's bed and roared out,—

"How are you getting on?"

The only reply was a low snore. He then turned to the boy and yelled the same question at him. The boy blinked and stretched, and then faintly gasped out that "he was a little better." Frantic with rage Bob bent down close to the old man's ear, and screamed out the same question to him again. The old chap stretched and yawned, and sleepily murmured,—

"Time to get up, sir? dear, dear!"

"You scoundrels," shouted old Bob. "I came up and saw you all talking;" and choking with rage, turned upon his heel and walked out of the room.

The following day Bob gave the doctor an account of the previous night's performance, but as the old man was really ill and his sentence would expire in a couple of days, and not, I suppose, feeling altogether satisfied about the boy, he declined to pack them all out of hospital, as Bob suggested, and decided to leave matters as they were for the present. The old man was well enough to go out on the day his sentence expired; and Bob, to encourage the boy, I presume, went up on the evening previous and congratulated the old chap on the fact, assuring him " that he was a very lucky fellow, and the first man he had ever known leave the hospital alive."

The following day the doctor, unable to discover what was the matter with the boy, concluded that he must be shamming, and ordered him back to his cell. A day or two later he was again found insensible on the floor of his cell, and the doctor sent for post-haste. Once more the youth was ordered back to hospital, and the doctor spent another week in trying to find out what was the matter with him. Baffled in his attempts, the doctor consulted with the governor and chief warder. The latter suggested that the boy should be taken out of bed, well flogged, and sent to hard labour. The governor, however, thought that although that sort of treatment might do in some cases, it was better to be on the safe side.

Finally, they decided that he should be medically treated for shamming, and this is how they set to work. On Thursday they applied a large blister to the nape of his neck, Friday a huge mustard plaister about the size of a small bed pillow was placed on the pit of his stomach, Saturday and Sunday they left him to enjoy the delights of these practical jokes, and on Monday, I believe, started at him with the stomach pump. What next happened to him I do not know, but on Wednesday the boy was still holding out, and the doctor was more nonplussed than ever.

The following week he once more decided that the boy was shamming, and sent him back to his cell with orders that he was to be treated as if he were perfectly well. On the Friday and Saturday I saw the boy in chapel, and he looked very far from well; this, perhaps, was no wonder after the shamming treatment, but there was a dazed, wild look about his eyes that gave me the impression of there being something wrong with him.

On Sunday Johns was unlocking the cell door, and looking into the boy's cell to see if he was getting up, saw him stretched stark naked on his plank-bed with his face covered with blood. Johns at once called out to one of the other officers to go and fetch the chief warder. As soon as the latter arrived he and Johns entered the cell and made an examination of the boy. The outside of the right thigh had a long, jagged wound in it, some six or seven inches long, which had bled considerably, as there was a large patch of blood soaked right through the mattress. He was unable to speak, and pointed to his throat, muttering something that sounded like glass. The doctor was immediately sent for, and on his arrival the boy's leg was carefully dressed (curiously enough it was about the only place on his body where he could have cut himself about in the way he had without doing himself some very serious, if not mortal injury); as it was the wound there was soon set to rights, but the state of his throat was a very different matter. He was quite unable to swallow anything, and was apparently suffering great pain; and no wonder, for little by little they got out of him that he had got hold of a medicine bottle there was in his cell, broken it, cut his leg with one of the fragments, and then set to work to eat the remainder of the bottle. His throat naturally objected to having this kind of thing stuffed down it, and some of the glass seems to have stuck in his gullet.

The governor came hurrying up while the doctor was examining his patient, and was in a tremendous rage with the boy, and told him he had a great mind to handcuff him. The chief tried to persuade the governor to order the boy three dozen with the cat-o'-nine-tails, but the doctor interfered and said it was nonsense to talk of anything of the kind, as the boy could not be in his right mind.

After breakfast the doctor again visited him, and tried to get some milk down his throat, but without success. The governor, who was again present, then solemnly demanded of the doctor "whether he couldn't cut the boy's throat and get out what was obstructing the passage." The doctor stared at him in silent amazement, and the governor, seeing his astonishment, continued, "and stick it together again afterwards, of course." The doctor, with praiseworthy gravity, replied, "Oh, I couldn't do that."

But the two warders, who were also in the cell, did not know what to do to keep from laughing, and half an hour later the story was all over the prison. It must have been pleasant for the unfortunate boy to have to listen and hear the governor quietly urging that his throat should be cut. He was sent back to the hospital, and after a bit the doctor got his throat and leg all right, but the boy still declared he was dreadfully ill, and they seemed as far as ever from knowing what really was, or had been, the matter with him. When my sentence expired he was still in hospital, and I believe he stuck up there until he had served his time.

I have now said enough, I think, to show that

the hospital regulations are far from perfect, and will return to my own experiences.

Now that I had discovered that it was old Bob who was persuading the doctor not to order me any extra diet I determined to alter my tactics, and instead of saying anything more to the doctor quietly sent for the chief warder, and had a talk to him. I did not say anything about old Bob, but simply told him that I was really in need of some kind of extra food, which the doctor did not seem inclined to grant me, and asked him what I had better do.

"Well, now, look here," he said, "you send for the doctor to-day and tell him the thing right out, just as you have told me, and I'll try and see him myself and tell him that you require some change."

The chief was as good as his word, and the same afternoon the doctor came down to my cell and ordered me a pint of new milk morning and evening, in lieu of gruel, and white bread in lieu of brown. A fortnight later he ordered me four ounces of cooked beef every Monday, in lieu of bacon and beans, and so as far as food was concerned, I now got on all right. The mat-making interested me and kept my mind employed to a certain extent, but after a couple of months I began to suffer serious inconvenience from the fine powdery dust with which the cocoa-nut fibre impregnates the air. It affected my chest and throat, and began to trouble my lungs. I sent for the doctor, and he told me I might leave off mat-making if I chose, but I declined this offer, as I should have been stranded with nothing to do. I told him I would go on with it for the present, and then as soon as the first twelve weeks of my sentence were over, which would be in about another month, and I was eligible for employment of trust in the prison, I would apply to the governor to let me have some writing to do.

On the first occasion of the visiting magistrates' monthly inspection, I got hold of the chairman and asked him if he would allow me to have a tooth-brush in my cell. On learning that I had one amongst my things in the store room, he at once gave me leave to have it. Emboldened by my success I then asked him if

I might have a cold bath once or twice a week; but after referring to the governor he informed me he had no power to make an order for this, but advised me to apply to the doctor. This I had already done, with the result that the doctor said "he had no objection if the governor hadn't." And on my applying to the governor, he said "he had no objection if the doctor hadn't;" but between them I could not get my bath.

I gave up all thoughts of the bath in despair on learning that the magistrates had no power to order me one; but my mourning was soon turned into joy, for a couple of days later the doctor came down to see me, and told me that I should have a bath twice a week. So I suppose that the chairman, as nice an old man as ever stepped, gave the doctor a hint.

Here again Bob interfered, imagining that I should require a hot bath, and knowing that this would give him the trouble of seeing after it, he persuaded the doctor to make an order for only one bath a week. On discovering this I sent for the doctor, and told him he had promised to let me have two baths a week, and Bob, having now found out that I wanted them cold, and that consequently it would give him no trouble as I could fill the bath myself, withdrew his opposition, and the doctor made the necessary order.

A few weeks later I got him to alter it to three baths a week, and between being thus enabled to keep myself clean and the daily quart of new milk, I rapidly regained strength.

The bathing arrangements for the prisoners at Xshire were simply abominable. The Government regulations say "that the prisoners shall be bathed at such times as the governor may direct, provided always that they shall have a bath at *least* every 15 days." This is surely seldom enough; but at Xshire this regulation was systematically broken, and the prisoners were bathed, on an average, about once in five weeks.

I kept a record of the bathing days in my diary, and am therefore enabled to give exact data on this matter.

Some idea of the irregularity of the bathing

will be gathered from the following:—" From January 9th to March 4th the prisoners were only once bathed, viz. on February 6th. Now within that period the *minimum* number of baths they were entitled to, according to the Government regulations, would have been three. This was chiefly the fault of the engineer, who was a lazy fellow, and objected to taking the trouble to see that the water was heated, as this necessitated his attending to the boiler for an hour or so; and whenever bathing day came round, he had always forgotten to heat the water, and so it was put off another week, and then the same excuse was made once more.

Of course if the chief warder had done his duty he would very soon have stopped this kind of thing; but the engineer used to do all kinds of odd jobs for him, so he did not interfere.

The bathing, even when it did take place, was so scandalously managed that it was a disgrace to a civilized country, and, as a rule, sent the men back to their cells dirtier than they were before, and in many cases covered with vermin.

A short account of a bathing day at Xshire will, however, do more towards showing people the disgusting nature of the arrangements than anything I could say. There were two bath rooms situated opposite one another in a small alcove between D corridor and the receiving ward. They each contained a slate bath some seven feet long by about three broad and three deep. The two bath-room doors were thrown open, a curtain was run up on each side of the passage, leaving a narrow space curtained off close to each bath-room door, and in this space the men were supposed to undress. In the central passage between the curtains were stationed a couple of warders, one superintending one bath, and the other the opposite one, while in the C corridor there was a third warder ready to let the prisoners out of the cells when the baths were duly prepared. As soon as this was the case one of the warders would step out to the bottom of the staircase and call out to the one in C, "Bath ready, send down two men." This warder would then unlock a couple of cells, call to the occupants, "Bathing; off with your jacket and waistcoat, take your towel, and go down." On arriving at the bath-room the men would pass behind the curtain, throw off their clothes, take a large piece of soap, and spring into the bath. They would be no sooner in than the warder would immediately call out, "Two more." By the time they arrived the other two were supposed to be out and drying themselves, and whilst the new comers took off their things the others were supposed to complete their drying and be ready to pass from the bath room behind the curtains, and leave the baths vacant for the new arrivals. The same thing went on all the afternoon, the corridors re-echoing with the continual cry of "Two more."

Some idea of the pace at which this so-called bathing was carried on may be gathered by comparing the number of men bathed with the time expended. The daily average number of male prisoners was about 120; the bathing commenced at two o'clock, and usually finished at half-past four. There being sixty men to each bath, this would just give an average of two and a half minutes per man; and I imagine a fellow would have to be pretty smart to undress, bathe, and dress in the time. Still they did it somehow or the other, for the warders made every man get into the bath and soap himself. In they went, one after the other, no matter what some of them might have the matter with them; and in prisons there are almost invariably a fair number of ulcered legs, boils, blains, running sores, itch, lice, and venereal cases; but it all went in together and made a nice mixture.

The water was changed *once* during the course of the afternoon, so that thirty men, diseases and all, went into each bath, and the water must have been in a nice condition after about twenty of them had left their varied impurities in it.

No one who had not seen it could imagine the state the water became in; pea-soup is the only thing that will give any idea of it, and how such a state of things can have been allowed to exist in a Government establishment, month after month, year after year, is "one of those things that no fellar can understand." But it is too serious a matter to joke about, for anything more disgusting, anything more filthy, or more utterly subversive of all decency and respectability, it would be impossible to conceive.

There were always about nine or ten bars of soap drawn from the stores for bathing day; about two of them, or at the outside three, were used by the prisoners, and the remaining six or seven bars were quietly walked out to the wheelhouse (at least such was the report) to be thereafter divided between Humphrey and old Bob; so that *they* did not trouble themselves to buy any soap for their families from one year's end to the other.

As the doctor had ordered me cold baths I escaped all the horrors of this regulation bathing; and how thankful I felt when I saw the kind of business it was!

The days now passed away in an unbroken monotony, and the description of one day will do for the whole three months.

At five minutes past six in the morning the rising bell rang; by half-past, one was dressed and had the cell swept up and hammock rolled and stowed away on its shelf. As I was not tasked I did not commence work until seven, at which hour I used to get my mat frame upon the stool and set to work. At 7.45 breakfast was served, and at half-past eight the warder came round to collect the mess tins for dinner, and I then used to recommence work. About ten minutes to nine the banging of the doors would warn me that the governor was on his way round, and then on went your stock and you stood to attention in the middle of the cell, ready to salute when the corridor warder threw open your door and the little man marched by. If you had any complaint or request to make, you took one pace to the front as he arrived at your door, and he would then stop and hear what you had to say. This performance over, one set to work again until twenty minutes past eleven, when the bell rang for prayers, and the prisoners were marched in single file, three paces apart, up to the chapel. Warders were stationed about to see that there was no attempt at talking among the prisoners; but the men always managed to talk somehow or the other, and I have been followed all up the corridor with the everlasting question, "How long have got?" Every now and then a man would get bowled out and be reported to the Governor, but considering the persistent way in which they talked, it was quite wonderful how seldom they were detected.

Habitual criminals have a way of talking without any perceptible movement of the lips, and throw their words out from the back of the throat in a ventriloquous kind of manner, rendering it exceedingly difficult for the warder to tell where the talking comes from, even should he happen to hear it.

It took some time to get the men all into their places, and the service commenced at twenty minutes to twelve, and by twelve o'clock we were all back in our cells ready for dinner.

This did not take one long to eat, and by half-past twelve I had usually finished mine and got my tins washed and ready to pass out for supper. Dinner over, I used to read (when my first two months were over and I was allowed library books) until half-past one, at which hour the warder came round and collected the mess-tins for supper, and then I resumed my work. At two o'clock I used to go out to exercise for an hour—for having a bad leg and being unable to walk I got the doctor to make an order for me to exercise alone—and could move about in the little airing yard just as I pleased. If I had exercised with the rest of the prisoners I should have been obliged to march round and round at a fixed pace, with the usual three paces between each man.

The regulations say "that a prisoner shall have an hour's exercise daily;" but the way the regulations were carried out at Xshire was, to say the least of it, peculiar, and the men never got more than half an hour a day, and when old Bob exercised them, only twenty minutes.

Another great advantage I had was being allowed to take my exercise without any warder to look after me, for I was simply turned out to do as I pleased. The gate leading from D corridor was locked behind me, so that I could not get into the prison again until the warder came to fetch me; but the door beyond, at the end of the passage that ran between the cocoa-nut beating sheds, and which opened into the airing-ground itself, was usually left open, unless I chose to shut it, and I was consequently enabled to hear many a funny tale, and learn a great deal of useful information from the conversations held between the men who were engaged in shell beating.

Humphrey used to lend me a little stool, and I used to place this against the wall near the door as it was one of the sunniest spots, and here I used to sit in comfort enjoying all the advantages of the conversations that were carried on without rendering myself liable to any punishment; for I was scrupulously careful never to speak a word to any of the prisoners myself, for I was determined not to run the slightest risk of having the order for my exercising alone rescinded. And besides, I knew that the warders gave me a certain amount of extra liberty during my exercising hour on the tacit understanding that I would not abuse their confidence, and I was therefore bound in common decency to strictly observe the rules.

The oakum shed, as it was called, was a kind of lean-to built on to the end of the prison, and had originally been used for the oakum-picking gang, whence its name; but it had now been entirely altered, having been divided by brick partitions into some seven or eight small cells, in each of which a man was now employed in beating out the cocoa nut husks with a heavy hammer, so as to soften them sufficiently for other prisoners to pull into pieces. Each cell was furnished with a wooden block, a hammer, and a certain number of husks, and the prisoners engaged in the work were employed at it from half-past six in the morning until five o'clock at night, but were allowed, of course, a certain amount of time for their meals.

It was very hard, monotonous work, but the

prisoners were delighted to be employed at it as it gave them an opportunity for talking, of which they were not slow to avail themselves.

There was no warder to look after them. Humphrey placed them in their different cells, and then went off to attend to the treadwheel; and the door into D corridor being shut, the men always had timely notice of any warder's arrival, for they could always hear their keys jingling as they unlocked the doors.

The cells were situated on either side of a very narrow passage, the cell doors being exactly opposite to one another; and as there had been, for some reason or the other, a space of some seven or eight inches left between the bottom of the doors and the flooring of the cells, all the men had to do was to lie down on the floor, place their faces in the aperture, and then they could talk away as quietly as possible.

When there were only two or three men employed here, and Humphrey was cute enough to locate them in cells that were not *vis-à-vis*, it made very little difference, as the spy-holes in the doors were not glazed, and a man could push back the iron outer lid, and passing his little finger through the hole to keep the lid back, make a kind of tube with his hands round the hole that carried his words up and down the little passage as clearly as a bell.

This work was considered to be first class hard labour, and the men employed at it were invariably entered in the daily labour book under this heading; yet the men engaged at it while I was at Xshire were without exception either in the second, third, or fourth stage, and hence only allowed, according to the rules, to be employed in second class labour.

This was another instance of the peculiar manner in which they carried out the government regulations here. They had no more right to employ a man in the second stage on this kind of work than they would have had to make him go on the wheel; yet here were the regulations being daily broken, and the governor either ignorant of the manner in which the men under his charge were employed, or else permitting the rules to be broken.

The prisoners themselves, of course, made no complaints about the work, even if they knew they had a right to do so, which I very much doubt, as the opportunities for talking would more than counterbalance any amount of work in their eyes. Still, the thing was wrong, and the authorities paid for their neglect of the rules, for if they had employed men in the first stage as directed, there would have been none of the habitual talking that was carried on now; for in the rapid changes that this would have necessitated (a man only stopping in the first stage for twenty-eight days), the prisoners would never have had the time to learn all the ropes, and would have supposed that if there was not a warder near, one was likely to come along at any minute.

The thing that used to astonish me most was the manner in which the prisoners seemed to know all that was going on in the prison, and for a long time I could not make out how they obtained their information. They always knew, for instance, exactly how many new men had come in on the previous day, and what sentences they had got; and if any man had been punished by the governor they knew all about it, and what his sentence was.

When one of the shell beaters was getting near the end of his sentence, there would be all kinds of arrangements made for him to carry out letters for the friends and sweethearts of his less fortunate companions who had still some time to serve. Five shillings was the usual price charged for this accommodation, and the waistband of the man's drawers the favourite place of concealment for the letters. Where they got their paper and pencils from puzzled me, and I never could discover exactly how they managed it; but there is no doubt that they must, in most cases, have secreted the pencil somewhere about them on their first arrival whilst old Bob was putting them into their prison clothes; but although it was a notorious fact that letters were continually being passed about in chapel and during exercise, the warders never seemed able to discover where the paper and pencils came from. Apparently every precaution was taken, and if a warder happened to drop a piece of pencil by accident the prison was searched high and low until it was found, and yet there was hardly a prisoner who had not got a bit of pencil about him somewhere.

Sometimes, during my exercise hour, Humphrey would come through from the treadwheel and have a chat with me, and many a hearty laugh we had together. Humphrey had a whole pack of cleaners, and usually had one or two at his heels wherever he went; but the most extraordinary thing was the mania he had for selecting the most hideous-looking ruffians in the prison. Unless a man was either humpbacked, blind, crippled, or idiotic, Humphrey did not care to have him about him, excepting in one or two cases where the men's personal appearance happened to be so repulsively hideous that he consented to excuse their lack of bodily deformity.

My exercise was always a great pleasure to me, and I never shall forget how beautiful I thought the little dingy plat of grass looked when I came out for the first time after being shut up day and night in my cell for the requisite twenty-eight days that the authorities require you to undergo before permitting you to have any exercise.

Nobody who has not experienced it can imagine how beautiful the sky looks when one has seen nothing but four whitewashed walls for a month, and I thought the few daisies and buttercups sprinkled over the grass far exceeded in beauty any flowers I had ever seen before.

When a man is certified unfit for first class hard labour, he ought to be allowed exercise at once, for being mewed up in a cell without a book of any kind to relieve the terrible tediousness of the confinement must be a very great strain on the health of any man.

About a quarter-past three Johns would come and tell me that time was up, and I would then return to my cell and continue mat-making until 5.45, at which hour supper was served out. After supper I used to set to work once more at my mat, and keep at it till the clock struck seven; then, down went my mat-frame into its corner, my working materials were all stowed away in their appointed place, and after sweeping my cell I used to sit down and read until the bell rang at eight o'clock for us to go to bed. Other prisoners of course worked on steadily till the bell rang, but as the doctor had forbidden my being tasked I always stopped at seven; though I believe if the warders had wished to be disagreeable they might have made me keep on working at some light employment until bedtime. Nobody ever said a word to me; even Johns never went any further than to pop my trap down once or twice, and after a brief survey of the scene within, retire with an expressive snort of patient disgust, and so I always retained this hour for my own amusement. At five minutes past eight o'clock the warder on duty would come round and collect all the tools the men had been using for their work during the day. Each man's tools—these consisted of the scissors, hammers, sailmakers' needles, &c., used for mat-making—were placed outside his cell on the floor, and then when the warder came round the following morning to unlock the doors each man's tools were passed back to him again. Just before I left Xshire an order came down from the commissioners that a card was to be placed outside each man's door, containing a list of the tools he had in daily use; and a further order, that before a prisoner left his cell, either to go to chapel, exercise, or for any other purpose, he was to place his tools on the cell table, and the warder who let him out was supposed to see that they were all there. A few days later another order came down that whenever a warder, or any other prison official, opened a cell-door, the prisoner was immediately to lay any tool he had in his hands on the floor, and leave it there until the warder left the cell again. This last order was sent down in consequence of a warder in one of the Midland prisons having been nearly murdered by a prisoner, who attacked him, on his coming into his cell to give him some directions, with a pair of large mat-shears, and as nearly as possible knocked his brains out. At 8.30 the warder again came round to double-lock all the cell-doors, and to see the prisoners were in bed, and, that finished, made a third and final tour round the corridor, turning out the gas and violently thumping each door to make certain that it was duly fastened. One would have thought that these were precautions enough, but the authorities did not seem to think so, for at ten o'clock, when the night watchman came on duty, he used to go all round the prison, and re-inspect all the doors. At least this was what he was supposed to do, but as a matter of fact he had three or four pet doors in each corridor that he used to thump unmercifully, passing by the next without trying them at all. Unfortunately my door was one of his *protégés*, and every night, at about a quarter past ten I used to hear him come paddling along the coridor in his stocking feet, until he arrived at my cell-door, and then he used to relieve his feelings, and considerably disturb mine, by a sounding thwack on the door. He had another unhappy victim on the opposite side to me, and then he left all the rest of the prisoners in peace and quietness until he arrived at the far end of the corridor again, where he had another familiar friend. It was quite useless to go to sleep before he had been round, as he always woke me, so I never attempted to do so until I had got rid of him, but then I soon fell asleep; for a prison day is a very long day, a very weary day, and one longs for sleep, with its sweet oblivion of all the petty trials and annoyances that are of daily occurrence in a prisoner's life. Such was my daily routine for three long months, each day bringing the same monotonous round of duties—the same faces, same food, same everything. Twice a month we had a break in the prevailing sameness.

On the second Tuesday in each month the visiting justices came round to inspect the prison, hear complaints, and what they pleased to call transact business (which consisted of standing round the fire in the committee-room discussing the latest local gossip); and on the last Friday in the month the government inspector came down to inquire into the condition of the prison and issue new regulations. On both occasions a vast deal of preparation was made, the prisoners having to give their cells an extra washing out, and to carefully examine all their scanty furniture, and see that there were no spots or specks about it. Gradually, however, the preparations made for the former have been getting smaller and smaller, for since the prisons have been under government the powers of the visiting magistrates have been so extensively curtailed that it is difficult to see what they come to the prisons at all for. By stretching their authority to its utmost limits they came to the conclusion that they might allow me to have my toothbrush in my cell, but when I applied for leave to have a bath they decided that although they might allow a man to keep his teeth clean, it was quite beyond their power to give him permission to extend his ablutions any further. I tried hard to find out something that they would be empowered to order me, and for this reason was continually making applications to them, but never got beyond the tooth-brush. The only remnant of their ancient power that they still retain is the being able to order a prisoner to be flogged, if the governor brings one before them for any very gross breach of discipline. In old days their power was supreme, and they bitterly resent their present cipheric condition. It was just the kind of fussy, prying, old-womanish sort of work that was admirably adapted to the capabilities of the GREAT UNPAID. They had the appointing of all the prison officials, from the governor downwards, and the power of dismissing them if they did not suit, so they were of course treated with that extreme deference and respect that we instinctively pay to those upon whom our bread-and-butter depends. All this is now a thing of the past; and the authority originally vested in them has been handed over to the government inspector, and the deference of the warders has in a great measure been transferred with it. Formerly anything that the justices disapproved of became the subject of apologetic inquiries and explanations; now, any complaint they make is met with the stereotyped reply, "The matter shall be mentioned to the government inspector."

The poor old magistrates are dreadfully indignant at the present state of things, and have continually memorialized and interviewed the Home Secretary, but without avail. It seems a very great pity that when government had all these old fogies ready and anxious to do this visiting work for nothing, it should go to the expense of appointing a staff of prison inspectors at high salaries. It seems a still greater pity that the taxpayers should have to pay some 9000*l.* every year, when there is not the slightest necessity for it. I say there is no necessity for it, because I am perfectly satisfied that anyone who is acquainted with the practical working of the present system of inspectors would agree with me that there is no adequate gain for the money expended, either in the preventing of ill-treatment to the prisoner, or increased efficacy in the staff. On the contrary, affairs would be far better and, of course, more economically managed by reverting to the old system, and doing away with the inspectors altogether. Let us take Xshire Prison as a typical example of the two systems: Here there were twelve respectable county magistrates willing to give up one afternoon each month to an examination of the condition of their county prison. This committee comprised the eldest son of a peer, four baronets, five representatives of old county families, one retired doctor, and one banker; the latter's wealth being allowed, I suppose, in these plutocratic days, to make up for his want of blood; while the medical man had been very wisely placed on the committee as being, from his professional knowledge, able to form a correct opinion of the bodily health of the prisoners and the sanitary condition of the prison. I have perhaps been wrong in stating that the old gentlemen appointed the banker on account of his wealth, for I fancy they did it with an ulterior view to his capabilities in financial arithmetic, for they had no sooner got him on the committee than they made him secretary and treasurer, and, to his credit be it said, from that day forward their accounts became intelligible. The whole twelve did not of course come every Tuesday, but there were always six or seven of them. The social position of the large majority of the committee was in itself a guarantee that all inquiries and reports would meet with an honourable and straightforward examination, while their number insured a full and careful one. In addition to this numerical advantage they were far more likely to form an impartial opinion of any complaints made by the prisoners than government inspectors would be; for the latter have always previously held appointments in either the convict or prison service, and are naturally biased against the prisoner, and in favour of the governor. Their examination of the prison, too, was far more methodical and exact; and in addition to this, they used to arrive at the prison just before dinner-hour and lunched off a portion of the same food as was served to the prisoners. In this way the cook was obliged to prepare the food properly once a month, thus enabling the prisoners to discover if their meals were "up to regulation" on other days, as they only had to compare them with the "magistrates' Tuesday."

They used to listen to any complaints of ill-treatment made by prisoners with the greatest attention, and ask questions enough for a state trial; but in old days they were unfortunately rather prejudiced in the warder's favour, as he was sure to be some *protégé* of their own; but now that the government make all the appointments there would be very little fear of any miscarriage of justice on this score. They used to thoroughly examine the prison from top to toe when they came, and for a week beforehand the warders and prisoners would be scrubbing here, painting there, and polishing somewhere else, until there was not a spot in the whole place you might not have eaten your dinner off. A speck of dirt to them was like water to a mad dog, and some of them no doubt rode to death the hobby for cleanliness. One of the baronets, for instance, had a pleasing habit of spitting on his finger and then running it along the tops of the cell-doors, under the shelves, and various other out-of-the-way places that he imagined the prisoners might have omitted to clean. The banker, too, was inclined to go about the cells on all-fours, trying to find a scratch on the floor, or a piece of whitewash knocked off the wall. Fearful was the row in the prison when, on one occasion, the aforementioned baronet discovered a cobweb on the ceiling of a prisoner's cell! Oliver Twist's asking for more was nothing to it. Sir A—— B—— and the rest of his colleagues stood round the cell-door with uplifted hands at the depravity of a man who could be so lost, so base, so vile, as to have a "COBWEB—ACTUALLY A COBWEB!—ON HIS CEILING."

It is true that the cobweb was so small that they had to send for the clerk to bring a sheet of note-paper, in order that, being laid upon white paper, they might be the better able to inspect it. The size, however, did not alter the enormity of the offence, and Sir A—— had a written report made of the matter, and then ordered the cobweb to be enclosed in the sheet of paper and placed in the clerk's office among the other archives of the prison. The prisoner's punishment for this awful crime was, I believe, three days dark cell, and there was a serious consultation held as to the advisability of flogging him. Now, my readers must not suppose that this is any imaginary or exaggerated story; it is a simple statement of facts. Of course there will always be an ass or two on every committee, and where a committee was composed of county justices one would naturally expect a considerably larger number. And I am not at all sure that the asinine element is not a very useful one for the purpose of investigating complaints of alleged ill-treatment. There is a stubborn patience in the four-legged ass that is reproduced in his two-legged prototype in the form of an obstinate persistency to get to the bottom of a thing, and which takes no heed of trouble or time so long as it can hear itself talk, and eventually obtain, or imagine that it has obtained, the information it required. The advantage of this is, that it is exceedingly difficult for a man to answer a running stream of questions without contradicting himself, unless he is really telling the whole truth. A knave, too, is deceived by the apparent simplicity of the questioner, and, becoming over confident, makes some slip that is quickly seized upon by one of the other justices blessed with brains and common sense. At all events, with all their little weaknesses, the justices examined the prison thoroughly, entering every cell, and taking considerable trouble to inquire into all complaints that were made. The government inspector, on the contrary, used to dance through the prison in no time; attended by the governor and chief warder, and preceded by the warder of the corridor to unlock the cell-doors, he would come prancing along, and, as each door was opened, would just glance at the stage card, say, "Have you any complaints to make?" and, receiving a reply in the negative, pass at once to the next cell.

If any complaint was made by a prisoner the inspector immediately turned to the governor and asked him what he knew about it, and between them they dealt out a very summary kind of justice, and it was commonly stated, all over the prison, that if a prisoner made any complaint the governor was certain to punish him for some alleged breach of discipline before the week was out. Whether this was true or not I cannot say, but I do know this, that I on one occasion made a complaint to the inspector, and from that day forth the governor did what he could, in a quiet way, to make me uncomfortable. The circumstances of the case were sufficiently typical to deserve more than a passing notice, and I may as well give a brief account of them here.

After I had been at Xshire for some three months, Australian meat, preserved by salt, was served out for our Friday's dinner, in lieu of ordinary Australian beef, preserved by heat, that we had been in the habit of having. This new issue of salt beef was musty and bad, and, after carefully studying the government dietary, I came to the conclusion that the governor had no power to serve out salted Australian beef to us.

By referring to the dietary it will be seen that in the table of substitutes there is nothing whatever said about Colonial beef preserved by salt; the substitutes permitted in the list are, Colonial beef preserved by heat, and American, or other beef, preserved by cold. There is a special table concerning cooked salt meat, but that refers to ordinary English salt meat. The prisoners were all grumbling about the beef, and, as I was quite satisfied that the contractor had paid some of the officials a handsome percentage to accept it, I determined to have a talk with the chief warder about the matter, and, if that would not do, to appeal to the governor. On the first opportunity I had I mentioned the subject to the chief, telling him that the meat was salt, mouldy, and bad, and not at all equal to the meat we had been accustomed to have served out on Fridays; and that in addition I was perfectly satisfied that they had no authority to issue it.

"I know it's salt," he replied, "it's meant to be; it is corned beef, and I always consider that it is far better than the fresh, and, as a rule, the men prefer it."

I knew that this latter assertion was not

correct, but I could not tell him so, as he would naturally have wanted to know how I obtained the information. I pointed out to him though, that whether the prisoners preferred it or not had nothing to do with the matter, as it was not a question of what they preferred, but of whether the government regulations permitted the authorities to issue salt Australian meat, and that, although the prisoners might prefer chicken and ham, it could not be given them, because it was not on the dietary, and as they could not have what they would like they had no business to be forced to accept what they did not like.

"Wait a moment," he said, "I will go and get a dietary card."

In a few moments he returned with a large office dictary in his hand, and I pointed out to him the clauses I had referred to.

"You will see that there is a special table with regard to cooked salt meat there," I said; "but that refers to English salt meat."

"Yes, I know that," he replied; and having established this fact, I proceeded to attack him upon the quantity of meat issued.

"Well, then, even supposing you had a right to issue salt Australian beef, I am receiving a deficient quantity, as I should be entitled to $5\frac{5}{8}$ ounces every Friday, instead of the $3\frac{3}{4}$ ounces I at present receive."

"Why," he asked, "you are only in the third class?"

"Yes," I said; "but if you will refer to the dietary you will see that in that class of diet I am entitled to 3 ounces of English beef; but, if the authorities choose to substitute salt English beef I am entitled, by the table, to an increase of a quarter of an ounce per ounce, or $4\frac{1}{2}$ ounces in lieu of 3. Now, if this distinction is made between English meat, we are surely entitled to the same increase, if salt Colonial beef is issued instead of fresh Colonial, under these circumstances I should be entitled to $5\frac{5}{8}$ ounces of salt Colonial meat, as that would be the exact proportionate increase on the $3\frac{3}{4}$ ounces of fresh Colonial authorized by the table of substitutes."

He made no answer to this, but said he could not stop any longer, but he would think the matter over. On a subsequent occasion I again discussed the matter with him, but without avail, and, as the salt meat continued to be issued, and was apparently getting worse and worse, I appealed to the governor. I explained the state of things to him in the same way as I had previously done to the chief, but, although he had evidently—from his manner—discussed the matter with the chief, he simply said he would " see about it."

Whether he did see about it or not I have no means of knowing, but, if he did, he kept it to himself, for morning after morning passed without bringing me any answer to my application, and the salt meat was still issued.

I now decided to refer the matter to the government inspector; although I got several friendly hints from the warders that I had better leave the matter alone, or the governor would make it unpleasant for me. This, of course, only made me the more determined to carry out my intentions, for, if there was any truth in these reports, it was highly advisable for me to be made aware of it.

Accordingly, upon the next occurring visit

of the inspector, I made my complaint to him. He listened to what I had to say; asked to look at the dietary card, and then, turning to the governor, said, "Why do you give them salt meat?"

"Because the contractor sent it down," replied the latter.

"Very well," said the inspector turning to me, "I will talk the matter over with the governor."

What the result of the talking over was I never learned, but the salt meat continued to be issued until the supply sent down by the contractor was used up, and then we received fresh Colonial beef again, so that my application attained its aim in the end. I am sorry to say, however, that the personal results to myself were exactly in accordance with the hints I had received: my application to write an extra letter was refused, I was not allowed to continue the pleasant office work upon which I was now employed, but was ordered back to my cell to commence mat-making again. The doctor was asked by the governor to take away the extra food I was ordered and to replace me on the ordinary prison diet, and in a dozen different ways I was made to understand that I could not make successful complaints to the inspector with impunity. As the charge about the food is a grave one, I think I had better relate the exact circumstances that authorize me to make it. A week or two after the salt meat episode with the inspector, the doctor came down one night to my cell and asked me "How I was getting on?" I told him I was pretty well, and he then said,—

"Oh, by the way, do you think you could do without your milk?"

"No, sir," I replied, "I don't think I could."

"Well, you see the governor says the inspector does not like to see men getting extra food, and the governor asked me whether you could not do without your milk now and be replaced on the ordinary diet?"

"I don't see how I can, sir," I replied, "and if you will ask the warder of my corridor he will tell you that I eat hardly any of the food served out to me, and live entirely on my morning and evening allowance of bread and milk."

"To be sure, to be sure," answered the doctor; "you shall still have your milk. A man in your state of health requires some extra nourishment, and you shall have it."

So I kept my milk all right, but it was only thanks to the doctor, and although it may possibly have only been a curious coincidence, it is a very funny thing that no objections to the milk were made before; and a still more extraordinary circumstance was, that at this very time there were some fourteen other men in the corridor on extra diet, but no alterations were made with regard to them, and they all continued to receive their extra allowance whether the inspector liked it or not. Now I feel pretty certain that if I had made a complaint of this kind to the visiting justices, they would have taken very good care that I did not suffer for it in any way. The very first visit the inspector made gave me conclusive evidence of the utter inability of his visits for preventing ill-treatment of prisoners by the warders. I noticed on the occasion of the visit in question, that the inspector stayed some moments in one of the upper cells of the corridor, and guessed there was a complaint being made. After he had completed his rounds I heard him sharply reprimanding one of the warders, though I could not be positive which of them it was (I am morally certain it was old Bob), for the row was going on at the far end of the corridor. I could hear, however, that the warder was trying to make some excuse; and then I heard the inspector, in a loud and angry tone, say, " Nonsense, you know perfectly well that you have no business to strike a prisoner on any pretence whatever;" then his voice sank again to its ordinary pitch, and I was unable to hear the rest of his remarks, although I could tell that he was still making it pretty hot for the warder. A few moments later there was total silence in the corridor, and the bang of the glass door leading into the office passage told me that the inspector had left. He had been gone about five minutes when I heard the warder come stamping across the corridor, dash open one of the cell-doors, and shout out in a furious voice, "You ungrateful young scoundrel, I'll teach you to tell the inspector;" then there was the thud, thud, of heavy blows or kicks, interrupted by a scream of agony, and followed by a succession of short spasmodic screams, evidently produced by intense pain. The cries re-echoed through the cells with a startling distinctness; and then sudden shrieks of " Oh, don't, sir; don't! don't! don't! " intermingled with the gruff voice of the warder, hoarse with passion, declaring, with many oaths, that " he'd teach the young scoundrel to tell of him," told me plainly enough that the unfortunate prisoner was being again knocked about. A few more muttered oaths, the slamming of the cell-door, and the shuffle of feet across the corridor, showed me that the warder had left the prisoner's cell and returned to the warder's office. The prisoner still continued to utter loud cries, intermingled with ejaculations of pain, and in a few moments I heard the warder go across again to the man's cell and declare with various fresh oaths that "he'd give the young ruffian a fresh dose, if he didn't keep quiet." While this parley was being carried on I heard the door from the office passage open, and the chief warder call out,—

"I won't have you ill treat that man; he has a right to complain, and you leave him alone."

The warder replied "that he didn't see why he was to put up with being reported," but the chief called out sharply and authoritatively,—

"Come out of that cell at once; if you don't I'll go straight to the governor."

Then I heard the cell-door slammed-to, and the warder muttering threats of future vengeance went back again to the warder's office; and meantime the chief warder called out again in a loud voice,—

"I won't have the man ill-treated; if I hear you go near his cell again I'll report you straight to the governor. Now be careful," he continued, "because I shall certainly keep my word."

Then the office door slammed again, and the chief had evidently returned to his other duties. Loud cries still proceeded from the prisoner's cell, and it was some time before they entirely ceased.

It will no doubt be said that the chief warder ought to have gone at once to the governor, but I venture to say that eight chief warders out of ten would have acted exactly as Watergate did. Again, it may be asked why the prisoner himself did not report the matter to the governor when the latter went his rounds the following morning, or to the inspector on the occasion of his next recurring visit?

The best answer to these questions is perhaps that neither of these courses was taken in the above case, and no doubt the arguments used by the warder, whether persuasive or threatening, to prevent the prisoner making any further stir about the matter would be equally efficacious in any parallel case that might arise. At all events, from whatever cause, it distinctly proves that the visit of the inspector is not the slightest protection to the prisoner. The very fact of a warder daring to commit such an open violation of all rules and regulations, proves beyond a doubt that the warder considered that he could behave as he did with perfect impunity, for he must have known that detection of the act would have resulted in his dismissal, and he would not have been likely to run the risk of such a severe punishment as this unless he had been perfectly satisfied in his own mind that there was virtually no risk to run. Here again I think satisfactory proof may be adduced that the visiting justices would be far more likely to prevent cases of this kind occurring than the inspector. In the first place, there are sure to be two or three sharp inquisitive fellows amongst their number, who, once a complaint of this kind is made against a warder, keep continually making inquiries about the conduct of the particular warder for months afterwards; secondly, there are sure to be one or two earnest men amongst them who make it their business to inquire most carefully and fully into all cases of ill-treatment, and, having nothing to do with any other prison but their own particular one, are enabled to concentrate their whole attention upon any case that comes under their notice requiring special watchfulness. Thirdly, three-fourths of the prisoners are sure to be natives of the county in which the prison they are in is situated, and consequently are certain to know, and be known, by some of the visiting magistrates, and if persistent ill-treatment was being carried on in the prison, it would be sure to leak out and come to the ears of the magistrates sooner or later, and once on their guard, they could easily discover the truth or falsehood of the report. In short, I maintain that with the magistrates ready and anxious to perform the work the prison commissioners require done, viz. the proper and satisfactory supervision of our local prisons, the continuance of the present staff of prison inspectors is a most unnecessary and useless expense to the country. Any additional supervision (if the government thought it necessary) might easily be arranged for, by letting the prison commissioner for the district visit each prison in his district once every three months, and such an arrangement as this would give every security that either the government or public could possibly think necessary. In addition it would be a real act of charity towards the commissioners themselves, for from all accounts they must often be very hard pushed for something to do, and as they get a thousand a year a-piece, they might just as well do something for their money. It is commonly reported in the prison service that the chairman of the commissioners (Sir E. du Cane) is such a glutton for work that he shuts himself up in a little private room at the Commissioners' Office in Parliament Street, and does all that is to be done himself; even to the issuing of the circulars, keeping his colleagues in a state of indignant inactivity, for they naturally resent being treated as mere ciphers.

The days slipped away somehow or the other, and as soon as the first three months were over, and I was "*eligible for employment of trust in the prison,*" I applied to the governor to know if I could be employed at office work, and received the usual answer of "I'll see about it;" but in this case he really did see about it, and a couple of mornings later told me there was some writing for me to do, and that he would give orders for me to commence my new work on the following Monday. When that day arrived I was let out of my cell after the governor had gone his rounds, and conducted to a fair-sized room adjoining the committee-room, and on the opposite side of the passage to the governor's and clerks' offices. It was furnished with a large leather-topped table and some half-dozen most comfortable chairs, and having a large window looking out upon the warders' garden, seemed a perfectly palatial abode after three months of cell life. I found the table covered with a mass of papers, and Wigan, the clerk, came in to show me what to do. It seemed the governor was having an alphabetical list made of the prisoners sent to this prison for the last twenty years, with the number of convictions recorded against each of them, and the date and number of the Criminal Registry in which all particulars of them might be found, if required. There had been a naval prisoner employed on the work for some three or four months, but he, poor fellow, having gone out of his mind, had been taken off to the Asylum, and from the mess he had left things in it was quite time they did take him there. In addition to this I had to write up the daily labour book; balance weekly the provision and extra diet books, and between whiles sort, examine, and arrange all the commitment warrants for the preceding four years. Later on I had to mount on boards the new rules and regulations issued for female prisoners; make copies of the governor's answers to official inquiries; draw up the daily percentage of the various religious sects in the prison (a return of which had been called for by the Home Secretary, and this necessitated of course a careful examination of the Criminal Register for the two preceding years); make out the monthly average of prisoners, male and female, with a list of the different kinds of work at which they were employed; draw and cut out on cardboard large letters to be nailed on mat frames, to enable the mat maker to insert names or letters in the centre of mats ordered for hotels or public buildings; examine all the library books, making a note of such as were torn, defaced, written on, or otherwise damaged; and a host of minor jobs.

I have made this brief enumeration as showing the ample means placed at my disposal for obtaining a thorough insight into the management of the prison and the ordinary treatment of prisoners, as well as being able to form a pretty correct opinion on the comparative merits of the late and present system of conducting prisons, with regard to the suppression of crime and economy of expenditure.

The balancing of the provision books used to be a most amusing performance; and if the store accounts are kept in the same manner in the rest of her Majesty's prisons, it is no wonder that Government finds it difficult to make them pay. I generally used to find that the cook had issued about forty pounds of bacon in the month, and yet, according to the book, only received from the storekeeper perhaps fourteen or fifteen pounds. It was the same with regard to several other items in the book; and when I drew Wigan's attention to these curious discrepancies, he would say, "Oh, never mind; I have forgotten to put down the last lot I issued to the cook, but I'll make it all right;" and the necessary amount was filled in and things made "all right."

The arranging of the commitment warrants employed me for some time, and most interesting work it was. Perhaps it may sound curious to hear such a seemingly prosaic thing as a commitment warrant called interesting; but it must be borne in mind that this document becomes the receptacle of all kinds of information concerning the prisoner. Any gross breaches of discipline committed by him are endorsed on the outside, and if he has been flogged, a little paragraph in red ink notifies the fact and states at what hour the punishment was inflicted, and gives the names of the officials who were present. Any serious illness he may have had whilst in prison is also stated here, and the number of days he was detained in hospital. If the police make any inquiries about him, or furnish any information concerning his past career, the documents are carefully folded up inside the warrant, together with any other letters of inquiry that may have been forwarded by his relations or friends. Again, should the prisoner write any letters that the governor considered it advisable to keep a copy of, or write any containing matter contrary to the rules and regulations, or should there be any correspondence with the Home Office about him (with regard to the advisability of discharging him, either on the score of ill-health, or for any other reason), all the various documents find their way into the seemingly inevitable warrant; and lastly, in the event of the man dying from natural causes or suffering the extreme penalty of the law, every particular is safely stowed away in the same receptacle. But even now I have not finished, for his stage paper (containing the number of marks he earned and the labour he was employed at), his door-card, with his name, age, trade, &c., and the number of times, if any, that he had been reported to the governor, and the printed description-paper filled in by the receiving warder on the prisoner's admission, containing an exact description of his personal appearance, distinctive marks, number of previous convictions, and a host of minor particulars, were also carefully folded up and placed inside the warrant.

One of these warrants could not be found, and I had to go through the whole lot, carefully opening and examining every paper they contained. Whilst engaged at this work I came across some most curious records; and as I kept a diary, in which I carefully noted down all cases of interest, I have thoroughly reliable data to refer to. Some of the letters addressed to the governor by the relatives of prisoners were most ludicrous.

One old woman sent a letter, offering the governor a nice fat canary bird if he would be kind to her son, and addressed the letter to "Mr. The Turnkey." She wrote two or three other letters on the same subject, always holding out promises of the canary, with a bulletin of the bird's health at the time of writing. She invariably finished her letters with " Your humbler servant, M——W——. God bless you all!"

Another woman headed her letter "To the Guvnor," and commenced "Dear sir, I hope you excuse me call you such, but I don't know your name," and went on to ask if he would allow her, "as a broken-hearted niece," to send a quarter of a pound of snuff to her aunt, who had just been sent to prison.

Other letters were written in what is vulgarly called the high-falutin style, and had evidently involved considerable study of some cheap "Polite Letter Writer." Of this sort of letter the following specimen is a pretty fair sample :—

"Sir,—I should indeed feel much obliged if you would inform me per return how my unfortunate brother is getting on, and whether his health is impaired. I can assure you my family have felt it most keenly to know that he is in prison. It was through having got drunk, in consequence of having been falsely and maliciously informed that the young woman with whom he had been keeping company was receiving the addresses of another. I can assure you, sir, the lad has never had any reprimand, much less judgment, passed upon him by any one of civil authority before, and has always conducted himself well. I really hope that you will extend to him that kindness and consideration which your discretion will permit. Perhaps you will kindly inform me whether his incarceration involves hard labour."

The description of the gentleman undergoing the incarceration was as follows:—Trade, servant; age, twenty; degree of instruction, imperfect.

Another letter of this description commenced, "Dear sir, I hope you will pardon me thus addressing you, but I hope the feeling of an anxious parent will be an ample plea for the intrusion." After various inquiries after the health of her "dear boy," and a fervent request that an "enclosed epistle" might be given to him, the letter finished up with "Trusting in your generosity and urbanity."

The dear boy in question was an able-bodied seaman, aged twenty-seven, of H.M.S. J——, sent to prison for forty-two days' hard labour for " breaking out of his ship, taking a boat from alongside, and remaining absent twenty-one and a half hours."

Other letters there were of inexpressible sadness, and which, though rough, ill-written, and ill-spelt, had a world of pathos in the words of farewell that instinctively told one of the weary, heartsick craving to look once more on the face of the receiver—letters written by men dying alone, unwatched, uncared for, in the dreary prison hospital, without one loving word, one pitying look.

There were other letters, sadder even than these; letters that fascinated one with a shuddering morbid longing to know their contents; the last farewell letters of those who had been sentenced to death, and were shortly to suffer the last penalty of the law. There were some other letters that reflected very little credit on the magistrates and police concerned in the case. They were contained in the warrant of a woman named Thomas, aged twenty-two, single, an " unfortunate." She was brought before a Mr. L——, on the 11th of

February, accused of sleeping in an outhouse on the night of the 10th, convicted as a vagrant, and sentenced to seven days' hard labour. She was driven over to the prison in the police cart on the following day (the 12th of February), and on arrival was so ill that the governor sent for the doctor, who examined her, and reported that she was quite unfit for labour of any kind, and needed the greatest care to save her life; and yet the wretched woman had been sent here for trying to get a little shelter on a cold February night. She was placed on extra diet, and with the help of considerable attention on the part of the doctor and the matrons was sufficiently well to be discharged when the seven days had expired. Meantime, the police had written to inform the governor, as is customary in such cases, that they intended re-arresting her, and requesting him to let them know at what hour she would be discharged from prison. Being, I suppose, aware of this, the doctor endorsed her discharge as follows: " *P. Thomas was admitted into gaol very unwell, and in a state of great debility. It was for some time doubtful whether she would be sufficiently recovered for discharge when her sentence expired. She needs rest and medical treatment, being quite unfit for work.—Signed, ——, Xshire County Prison."*

On her discharge from the prison on the 18th of February, she was arrested by the superintendent of the F—— Borough Police, and, notwithstanding the medical certificate, taken off at once to F——, a town some forty miles distant, and necessitating a railway journey of nearly two hours. On her arrival, she was handed over to the county police and taken to the police-station. The same afternoon, February 18th, she was brought before the magistrates and sentenced to fourteen days' hard labour. She was then taken back to the police cells, to be removed on the following day to Xshire. When the next day arrived she was so ill that the local doctor had to be called in, and by his advice she was removed to the workhouse infirmary, where she remained until the 21st, when she was certified fit for removal, and sent off to Xshire under police escort. She was received at the prison on the afternoon of the 21st, and the warrant was endorsed: "*Received into the prison in an exhausted state the effect of fits.—Signed,* ——, *Surgeon, Xshire Prison.*"

Captain C——, who was at this time governor, was disgusted at the way in which the woman had been treated, and wrote to the borough magistrates complaining of the conduct of the police in the matter. The magistrates of course took the part of the police, declared there must be a mistake somewhere, and promised to communicate with the superintendent of the borough force and let the governor know the result.

A few days later a letter came from the mayor of the town, enclosing one he had received from the superintendent, saying that he (the mayor) "hoped the governor would see from the enclosed that there was no blame attaching to anybody; but that, on the contrary, the woman had been treated with every attention." Whether this would be the view of the case taken by an impartial person, can be easily judged by a little careful consideration of the following letter which was the enclosure referred to :—

"To the Mayor of F——.

"SIR,—I beg to acknowledge the receipt of your letter containing a complaint made by the governor of the Xshire Prison with regard to the treatment of the woman Thomas. I re-arrested the woman on her discharge from prison, and then brought her down by rail to F——. As long as she was in my hands she appeared to be quite well; but a short time after I had handed her over to the county police she was taken with a fit, and remained so, more or less, the remainder of that day and the following night. The next morning, Tuesday, 19th inst., she appeared much better, and Dr. B—— advised her being removed to the Union, where she remained until the morning of Thursday, 21st inst., when, at her own special request and with the sanction of Dr. B——, she was removed to Xshire."

The letter finished up with an attempt at an injured-innocence kind of grumble that the governor of Xshire Prison should presume to suppose that a member of the police force could do wrong.

The question one naturally asks after the perusal of the above letter is: if the woman was " taken with a fit, and remained so, more or less, the remainder of the day " (whatever that may mean), how and when was she brought before the magistrates? The date of the warrant proves that she was before them on the 18th of February, and it makes one curious to know whether she was " more or less in a fit " whilst her case was going on, and if so, whether the magistrates considered fourteen days' hard labour good for fits.

The F—— magistrates had already earned an unenviable notoriety among merchant seamen, for it was openly asserted that they invariably convicted any disobedient seamen that were brought before them, with an utter disregard of both evidence and justice.

While I was at Xshire, they, on one occasion, convicted six seamen of disobedience, and sentenced them to six weeks' hard labour apiece; but after the men had been in the prison for four or five days, an order was sent down from the Home Secretary for the release of the whole lot.

Before Plimsoll's Act was passed these amiable justices used to be in their glory, and while the winter gales were blowing, as many as thirty and forty disobedient seamen a week were sent up to the prison by these glorious specimens of the Great Unpaid.

It was very curious the mania some people (they were almost invariably women) seemed to have for writing letters to prisoners that they had never seen or heard of. They were, as a rule, prosy moral lectures of the most commonplace description, and usually came enclosed with a pink note to the governor, containing a request that the prisoner might be allowed to have the letter if he (the governor) considered that a word in season would be beneficial.

These kind of letters of course always found their way into the warrant, for when the prisoner became entitled to a letter he was pretty nearly certain to have one from his friends, and being only allowed to receive one letter, he of course declined to have anything to do with his fair unknown correspondent. There were some other letters of somewhat the same description, but which might perhaps have done great and lasting good; earnest, hearty Christian letters, written by sensible people who, without knowing the prisoner personally. knew something about his or her past life, and being aware that the prisoner in question was orphaned or friendless, sent the letter to the governor with a request that if So-and-So did not get a letter when the time arrived for him to be permitted to have one, they would be much obliged if he would let the prisoner have the enclosed. Another curious thing was the number of people in England who must have missing relations, for a man who had died in the prison after refusing to give any name to the magistrates, and without the police being able to identify him, had his warrant full of letters from all parts of England with inquiries from people anxious to know if he could be the relation they were in search of.

There were other things, however, besides letters in the warrants, and the written reports of the trial of two seamen named FitzGibbon and Austen, who were brought before the visiting committee charged with mutiny and threatening to strike a warder, were very instructive, and from the careful inquiries I made about the cases, proved how easily a prisoner can be systematically ill-treated. Both of these men were, from all accounts, impudent, ill-tempered fellows, but that was no excuse for the persistently unfair manner in which the warders treated them. They were here while the prison was still under the county authorities, and in those days if a warder had a grudge against a man he could get him kept working at the treadwheel during the whole of his sentence, for rule 12 of the county regulations enacted that " Every male prisoner of sixteen years and upwards, sentenced to hard labour for more than fourteen days, is to be kept during the whole of his sentence at hard labour of the first class, for such number of hours, not more than ten, nor less than six (exclusive of meals), as may be prescribed by the visiting justices, unless the surgeon certifies that he is unfit for such labour, or the visiting justices substitute, after the first three months of a prisoner's sentence, hard labour of the second class, or employment in the necessary service of the prison, as a reward for industry and good behaviour." All therefore a warder had to do was to complain that a prisoner was inattentive or idle, and the justices would of course keep him at wheel labour.

At that time Johns was always the warder in charge of the treadwheel gang, and he took one of his afore-mentioned dislikes to FitzGibbon, and was continually snarling and growling at him. Not content with thus showing his disapproval, he proceeded to make FitzGibbon do considerably more than his share of work on the wheel. This could be perfectly easily managed by making the same man go number one on the wheel every day, as number one is the first on and the last off, thus getting some five or six minutes' more work on each turn than the men at the other end of the line. The men were worked in relays, fifteen minutes on and fifteen off, so that unfortunate number one, calculating the average day's work at eight hours per day, had just one hour and a half more work than the rest. This fact was so well known that the order of sending out the treadwheel gang was alternately reversed, thus the man who went out first in the morning was sent out last in the afternoon. This arrangement, however, was easily nullified by Johns after the men had come out and taken their places on the wheel, as all he had to do was to order any man he disliked to change places with number one. And in this way he used to give FitzGibbon all this extra work week after week. The man repeatedly complained that he was being unfairly treated, but the old justices were informed that it made no difference whether a man was number one or not, and having once got the idea into their heads, nothing FitzGibbon could say could get it out.

At last FitzGibbon's patience gave out, and one afternoon, on Johns ordering him to change places and take number one, he rushed across the wheelhouse to where Johns was standing, shouting, " I have had enough of this, and I'll give you one." And he undoubtedly would have "given him one," but fortunately for Johns the miller warder, Humphrey, happened to be just passing through the wheelhouse, and with great presence of mind he sprang in front of Johns and warned FitzGibbon to keep off, or it would be the worse for him. This unexpected interference took FitzGibbon by surprise, and he stopped short in his infuriated rush. Johns, taking advantage of this diversion in his favour, sprang upon the platform and rang the bell communicating with the main building of the prison, and the chief warder and two or three subordinates were down at the wheelhouse in no time. The affair was reported to the governor, and on the next committee day FitzGibbon was duly arraigned before the visiting justices. They listened to the evidence given by Johns and Humphrey, and then FitzGibbon was asked if he had any question to put to Mr. Johns. "Yes, he would like to ask him whether he had not treated him differently to any other prisoner." Johns replied "That he only obeyed orders, having received special orders to keep him (FitzGibbon) as much apart as possible from the rest of the prisoners." The chief warder was then examined to see what he had to say on the subject, and was more especially questioned as to whether number one on the wheel had more work to do than anybody else. This he denied, and said it made no difference, and on FitzGibbon asking him whether he considered that he had had fair play on the wheel, the chief in reply declared that he had been treated like any other man. Now whether the chief told a wilful and deliberate lie in making this answer, or whether he really believed he was speaking the truth, it is impossible to say, for I happen to know that he was exceedingly stupid about the wheel, and it was a long time before the warders could get him to understand that number one did, as a matter of fact, do a great deal more work than anybody else; but whether he was made to understand it before or after this present affair, I have no means of knowing. For Johns and Humphrey, however, there is not a shadow of excuse, as they both knew that the man had been most unfairly treated, but they both (although placed on their oath) refused to own it.

The result of the inquiry was that FitzGibbon was sentenced to be flogged, and received two dozen cuts with the birch.

Austen's case was much the same, and occurred about a month after the previous one. Johns had been bullying him in the same way, and one day while collecting a party of men, of whom Austen was one, to take over to do some washing, he was in a more than usually aggravating temper, and kept worrying and abusing Austen until the latter, losing all self-control, stepped up to him and said, " I am not going to be spoken to like a dog, and if you don't take care, I'll knock you down." Johns immediately called one of the other warders, and Austen was sent back to his cell and reported to the governor. On being brought before the justices he was also sentenced to a couple of dozen strokes with the birch. This is a most severe punishment, and the magistrates ought not to be empowered to order more than one dozen strokes. It is a most significant fact that although these two men (FitzGibbon and Austen) were both big, hardy, powerful men, seamen in the Royal Navy, they neither of them ever got over their castigation, and some five months later they were both liberated on the recommendation of the surgeon, who certified that they were both suffering from atrophy, without the slightest hope of ultimate recovery, and they were accordingly sent home to their friends to save the prison authorities the expense of burying them.

The treadwheel arrangements were all abominably badly managed, and one or two of the warders made a regular practice of using it as a means for paying off any man they had a grudge against, though I am bound to say that there were only one or two of them who were dishonest enough to lend themselves to this kind of work; and, luckily for the prisoners, Miller, the warder who succeeded Humphrey, was a good, honest, straightforward fellow, who treated the men kindly and fairly, and set his face against any attempt at injustice on the part of any of the other warders.

How very easy it is for prisoners to be improperly placed upon the wheel may be gathered from the fact that I found from the warrant of a boy named Rowe that, although under sixteen years of age, he had been regularly worked on the treadwheel. In his description-paper he was entered as fifteen years of age, and on the name-card attached to his cell-door this was again stated to be his age; yet, with these figures staring them in the face, the warders sent him out day after day to the treadwheel. It is a great mistake that the commissioners do not state in the rules issued to prisoners that no boy under sixteen years of age is to be employed at hard labour of the first class: it is not sufficient to issue this regulation to the governors and warders, the latter will take advantage of the ignorance of prisoners; in fact, the absurd things little boys are sent to prison for, and the way they are treated when they get there, is one of the most disgraceful features in our criminal prison codes.

The present agitation with regard to juvenile offenders was most urgently needed, and wherever Sir Vernon Harcourt got his information from, he struck the right nail on the head, and cut at the very root of the evil when he determined to stop the manufacture of criminals by preventing any booby of a justice from sending children to prison for little trifling offences that would be amply and properly punished by a good whipping. The Home Secretary has made a mistake, however, in applying to the county magistrates for advice on the subject, for they are about the only class of people in England who advocate the imprisonment of children for so-called offences against the law; and until the administration of the criminal laws are taken out of their hands and placed in the hands of men who are properly qualified for the work, there always will be injustices and absurdities committed.

One most brilliant example of justices' justice came under my notice, and as all the papers afterwards passed through my hands, I was able to form a pretty fair opinion of the case.

Two little boys named F—— and W——, aged respectively thirteen and twelve, were sent to the prison, and as one of them had the cell directly under mine, and used to howl all day long, to my infinite annoyance, I naturally felt a good deal of curiosity about him. The persistent way in which he howled was perfectly appalling, and he would keep steadily at it for the whole day. Yet one could not feel angry with the boy, for there was a ring of genuine heart-felt sorrow in his voice that convinced one that it was not from mere temper or mischief that he kicked up this terrible hullabaloo.

His companion in misfortune had a cell exactly opposite, but he was perfectly quiet with the exception of occasionally starting a conversation with his friend in the vain hope of soothing him.

On one occasion the howler had evidently reduced himself to a state of desperation, for I heard him call across to his friend,—

"'Enery! 'Enery!"

"What do 'ee want?" replied Henry.

"If I die will you die?" groaned the howler.

This pathetic appeal was stoutly and promptly

refused by Henry, who was proceeding to expostulate with his friend, when one of the warders arrived on the scene and informed the boys if they were caught talking again they would go into the black hole.

They tried in various ways to get the boy to stop howling, but without the slightest effect; and on setting a few inquiries on foot about the cause of this continually crying, I was told that the boy was not crying over his own troubles, but at the thought of what his mother and little brothers and sisters would do without him, as it seemed that it was on this child's earnings as a ploughboy and farm labourer that the family depended for their daily bread, for they had no father.

The two boys had been charged before a couple of county justices with stealing some strawberries from a garden, and sentenced to one month's imprisonment and three years' reformatory each. There were no previous convictions against them whatever, and yet for this trifling offence—and I maintain it was a trifling offence for boys in that position of life to yield to the temptation of jumping over a hedge to pick a few ripe strawberries—these wise justices solemnly put their heads together and sent the boys to prison.

If one examines the case a little, one sees what a cruelly idiotic course it was to take. Here was this boy F—— earning his daily bread, not idling about, and mainly contributing to the support of his mother and the younger children, yet they send him to prison; and, not content with that, pack him off to a reformatory for three years, as if he had been an idle young vagabond everlastingly getting into trouble.

His mother would now, of course, be thrown on the parish for support, and in addition the parish would have to pay the reformatory authorities 2s. 8d. a week for the three years the boy would be with them.

The other boy W——, only twelve, and crippled in one leg, was not likely to have been earning his livelihood, but it would have been far better to have given his family 2s. 8d. a week to keep him at home than to have tainted him with prison life, and sent him away amongst a lot of reckless young scamps at a reformatory.

There was another case, almost equally as bad, of two other little boys, Brown and Smith, only eleven years of age. They had been errand boys to a draper in a neighbouring town, and Brown had stolen six sheets, and Smith one. They were brought before the borough magistrates, and sentenced to three months' imprisonment, and twelve strokes with a birch rod.

Now these, perhaps, were cases for a reformatory, but sending them to prison was simple ruin; at all events, I am afraid it was to Smith, for he was employed shell beating in the oakum shed, and got talking with the other prisoners, and, from what I used to overhear going on, he got nicely grounded in vice long before his three months were up. At the expiration of his sentence Smith went out, carrying with him letters for two of the prisoners (one of them an habitual criminal) with whom he used to talk while employed in the oakum shed, and you may be quite certain that the sort of people he took the letter to would do their best to get hold of such a smart, nice-looking little chap as he was.

Another boy of fourteen years of age, who had been sentenced to three months' imprisonment for stealing 2*l.* from his employer, was also employed at this shell beating, and learnt no end of evil from talking with habitual criminals employed at the same work. I have previously explained how the prisoners managed to talk to each other while at work in the oakum shed, but it was particularly aggravating to see boys sent down to work there when one knew that shell beating was classed as first class hard labour, and that therefore no boy under sixteen had any right to be employed at it. I believe myself that the reformatories are very little better than the prisons, as far as weaning boys from crime is concerned, and it would be a considerable step in the right direction if government would pass a bill that only utterly incorrigible boys were in future to be sent to these places.

Why cannot the government start an industrial school on the same lines as the one started near Bruges by the Belgian Government for homeless, friendless, and troublesome boys, and which pays all expenses, and, in addition, a very handsome percentage on the money expended by the Belgian Government in founding it? When a man has been manufactured into an habitual criminal, it is astonishing the sum of money he costs the country, especially if he only goes in for petty offences. I came across one man in the Criminal Registry who had been sent to the Xshire Prison no less than sixty-five times in the last twenty years, and had never had a longer sentence than three months passed on him. His usual term was a calendar month. Now, think what that man must have cost the country in the way of witnesses, law costs, and travelling expenses, to say nothing of the expense of keeping him in prison for four or five months in each year, when, being a short sentence man, he would be employed at unremunerative wheel labour, and thus earn nothing at all towards his board and lodging.

There was another case of this sort, where a woman had been seventy-three times in the prison during the last fifteen years. I also had ample means of seeing the utter uselessness of attempting to prevent the so-called "social evil" by imprisoning "unfortunates," and I will give one fairly typical case of the many that came under my notice while arranging and classifying the commitment warrants.

Catherine P——, aged seventeen, occupation none (an unfortunate). Religion, Wesleyan; convicted for vagrancy on the 25th of June, 1872, and sentenced to fourteen days' hard labour. Discharged from prison 9th of July. Committed for stealing clothes, 17th of July, 1872, tried at the summer assizes, and sentenced to three calendar months' hard labour. Discharged on the 25th of October, 1872. On the 30th of November, 1872, "being an unfortunate," did behave, in St. Nicholas Street, in an indecent manner; sentenced to one calendar month's hard labour. Discharged on the 1st of January, 1873. On the 6th of January, 1873, being an "unfortunate," did behave in an indecent and disorderly manner, and, having been previously convicted of being an idle and disorderly person within the meaning of the Act, was sentenced to two calendar months' hard labour. Discharged the 6th March, 1873. On the 16th of March, 1873, an unfortunate, loitering and importuning, fourteen days' hard labour. Discharged 29th of March, 1873 (30th, Sunday). On the 31st of March, 1873, being a rogue and vagabond, behaved in an indecent and riotous manner in the public highway; sentenced to three calendar months' hard labour. Discharged on the 30th of June, 1873.

Now, here was this girl, convicted no less than six times within a year, and I have not the least doubt that she has been going on at about the same rate ever since. Now, these are the sort of people that want to be sent to a reformatory, for, if they could be kept to steady work until they had formed habits of industry, and were then placed in respectable situations, there is not the slightest doubt that the number of these most truly unfortunate people would be sensibly diminished in a comparatively short space of time.

The expenses of such an institution as I have mentioned need not be very great, and would, at all events, be far more economical to Government than the present system of sending these poor creatures to prison for the best part of each year. The great mistake made by the well meaning but intensely stupid people who have tried to legislate against this growing evil has been that they have wilfully shut their eyes to the fact that this kind of thing *will go on*, and have always aimed at introducing repressive measures instead of trying to keep within bounds what is unfortunately considered by the great majority of the world to be a "necessary evil." I have studied the question very closely in all parts of the globe, and discussed the matter with men of every shade of opinion, and always came to the same conclusion—that repressive measures are worse than useless, and that the only wise course to pursue is to keep the existing evil as far as possible within bounds, and direct all attempts at legislation to stopping the future supply of the raw material.

While looking over the Criminal Registry I was struck by the intense mania displayed by the criminal community for tattooing their persons with all kinds of eccentric devices. One would naturally imagine that they would be the very last people in the world to cover themselves with distinctive marks which it would be impossible to erase, and by which they could so easily be traced. Yet there was scarcely a prisoner without tattoos of some kind on him, and the majority were covered with them. Some of the subjects chosen were exceedingly curious; one man, amongst numerous other pictures, was described as having his right forearm tattooed with a seaman on a rum cask and a tombstone. While employed at this office work time passed away very quickly, and the work I had to do was mere play. I used to go up to my office at nine o'clock in the morning and work till 11.20, when the warder would come and fetch me for chapel. Service over, I went back to my cell for dinner, and as soon as I had finished this meal I used to read (the schoolmaster kept me well supplied with library books) until two o'clock, when I was turned out for my hour's exercise. At three I returned to the office and worked until 5.30, at which hour my work was over for the day and I went back to my cell for supper, and was left to pass the remainder of the evening how I pleased. The evenings certainly were rather long, but if I got tired I went to bed without waiting for the bell to ring as none of the warders ever made any objection. Once a fortnight I had the schoolmaster in to give me the fifteen minutes schooling I was entitled to, and as I did not require any instruction from him we used to pass the time in conversation. This was a great boon, for the continual silence becomes terribly irksome after a certain time. I often grumbled bitterly to the schoolmaster at his not giving me the fifteen minutes every week, which I was really entitled to according to the government regulations, but he assured me that it was impossible for him to visit a man more than once a fortnight as he was employed at office work all the day, and only had from six to eight on five evenings a week for instructing the prisoners. I still look back with lively gratitude to him for the kind and considerate manner in which he always treated me, and the unassuming good nature with which he gave himself a considerable amount of extra trouble to keep me well supplied with readable books. He was an honest, decent fellow, and all the time I was at the prison I never heard a prisoner say a word against him, although I know he reported several of them. One thing that greatly struck me, while looking over the commitment warrants, was the very trifling offences for which naval men were sent to prison, and although the grandiloquent style in which the offence was recounted made you for a moment fancy that some really grave misdemeanour had been committed, if you just put the rigmarole into sensible English the sentence passed seemed altogether out of proportion to the crime committed. Take, for instance, the following:—John Smith, found guilty of breaking out of his ship, stealing a boat from alongside, going ashore, and remaining absent 21½ hours; sentenced to 156 days' (six lunar months) hard labour. The plain English of this was that the man, seeing an empty shore boat lying handy, quietly dropped into her from one of the port-holes, rowed ashore, and after spreeing about for the best part of a day and night, quietly returned to the dockyard, gave himself up to the police, and was re-conducted on board his ship. He had handsomely paid the owner of the shore boat for leaving his craft in such a handy position (a lucrative business is carried on by the port boatmen by "forgetting" their boats close to the men-of-war), so that all John Smith had really done was to yield to the sudden temptation of getting ashore for a short spell. Take a still harder case :—John Brown, stoker, aged twenty-six; offence, striking his superior officer, sentence, twelve months' hard labour. Brown was the son of most respectable parents, but instead of staying at home and entering his father's business, most foolishly ran away from school at the age of fourteen, and entered as "a boy" in the Royal Navy. After doing two years before the mast, he came to the conclusion that stoking would suit him better, as the pay was considerably higher, and being a strong powerful young fellow had no difficulty in exchanging into this branch of the service. He liked the sea and got on capitally for ten years, and then one unlucky afternoon got leave to go on shore at Gibraltar, returned the worse for liquor, fell foul of one of the engineers (an ill-tempered, bullying fellow), knocked him down, and not content with this, on the chief petty officer coming to the engineer's assistance, he knocked him down too. He was of course very soon secured and placed in the guard-room. He was tried by court-martial, and in consideration of the exceptionally good character he bore was *let off* with twelve months. Brown's case was rendered still harder from the fact that he had been a steady, industrious man, and was engaged to be married to a most respectable girl, who, as soon as she learned that he was in prison broke off the engagement, as her friends very naturally objected to her marrying a man who had been in prison. Of course, everybody knows that discipline must be maintained, but where men, after great provocation, strike a blow in the sudden heat of passion, or weakly yield to the temptation (a great one to a sailor) of getting ashore for a few hours, it seems most unjust and unfair to treat them like criminals and place them in common prisons. Where sailors are convicted of theft or other crimes rendering them amenable to the criminal law of the land, one would have no objection to their being treated like the rest of her Majesty's subjects, but where the offences committed are simply and solely crimes because they happen to be contrary to naval discipline and good order, the men ought to be sent to the naval prisons only.

Seamen are continually being convicted for using insulting language to, or striking their superior officers. More than half the seamen that find their way into prison come for one or other of these offences. Superior officer has an imposing sound about it, and a civilian would most probably imagine that one of the lieutenants of the ship or at all events one of the midshipmen had been the object of the assault. Cases of this kind however are extremely rare, and the " superior officer" is almost invariably one of the numerous petty officers that the crew of a man-of-war are so plentifully sub-divided into. As a rule, it is some " officer" who a few months before was a comrade of the offender, and who now, proud of his newly-received authority, struts about bullying and nagging at men able to knock him into a cocked-hat in a fair stand-up fight. Of course this kind of thing must be put down, but let men be sent to the naval prison for offences of this kind. What is still more unfair to seamen is that two men may be found guilty of precisely the same offence, and one will get sent to a civil prison to undergo the punishment awarded him, while the other will undergo his at the naval prison. Under these circumstances the one man would be twice as severely punished as the other, for the diet and treatment of men in the naval prison is a very different thing to the way they are fed and treated in the civil prisons. At the naval prison at Lewes (at present I believe the only naval prison in England) the prisoners are fairly well fed, and treated in quite a rational manner. The dietary there is as follows :—

DIETARY FOR PRISONERS AT THE NAVAL PRISON, LEWES.

Breakfast	Sunday, Tuesday, and Thursday	Oatmeal Porridge	2 Pints.
		Milk	½ Pint.
Ditto	Monday, Wednesday, Friday, and Saturday	Oatmeal Porridge	2½ Pints.
		Milk	½ Pint.
Dinner	Sunday, Tuesday, and Thursday	Beef without Bone (weighed after cooking).	8 oz.
		Soup	1 Pint.
		Potatoes	1 lb.
Ditto	Monday, Wednesday, Friday, and Saturday	Indian Meal Porridge	3 Pints.
		Milk	½ Pint.
Supper	Sunday, Tuesday, and Thursday	Bread	8 oz.
		Milk	½ Pint.
Ditto	Monday, Wednesday, Friday, and Saturday	Bread	12 oz.
		Milk	½ Pint.

On Sundays, first class prisoners to have ten ounces of beef with soup and potatoes as above.

Men whose sentences do not exceed forty-two days to have two *meat* dinners a week, and Indian meal porridge on remaining five days.

Half a pint of porridge less at each meal that porridge is served, to all men before the expiration of the first fifty-six days of their sentence.

Sixteen ounces of bread in lieu of three pints of Indian meal porridge at the expiration of twelve months to prisoners in the first class.

By comparing the above dietary with the one I have previously given it will at once be seen how infinitely better the men are fed at the naval prison. The manner of treating the prisoners too differs considerably, the confinement being made far less irksome; for the men meet in a large workshop every day and do their work together, and although talking is strictly prohibited a very fair amount of it goes on in a quiet way. The work consists of bending hawsers, turning and fitting blocks, making fenders and various other nautical requisites. The most unpleasant feature of the place is the shot drill, an idiotic and senseles form of labour chiefly designed one would think with a view of rupturing men. During the first part of their sentence men have to pass an hour-and-a-half in the morning, and an hour-and-a-half in the afternoon, at this delightful employment, and I believe it is exceedingly hard work. It consists of stooping down (without bending the knees) and picking up a thirty-two pounder round shot, bringing it slowly up until it is on a level with the chest, then taking two steps to the right and replacing it on the ground again. This extremely simple operation is repeated until the hour-and-a-half is up. I once watched the prisoners at Lewes engaged in this cheerful amusement, and thought I had never seen such an idiotic waste of strength in my life. On the same occasion I went all over the prison and found it to be very clean and well managed, but the sanitary arrangements were far from perfect. It is a very small prison, and the want of sufficient accommodation here is the reason why the

Admiralty send the seamen and marines to civil prisons. It is a most false economy, and it would be far less expensive in the end if the Admiralty were to build another prison, or take over one of the existing civil prisons and turn it into a naval one. Under the present arrangement the men get injured in health by the scanty food and hard work, and their eyesight is almost certain to be permanently affected by the continual glare of the whitewashed walls of their cells. Men after they have undergone a sentence in a civil prison are quite unfit for hard work on board ship for at least a month or two (according to the length of the sentence they have undergone), and long sentence men are almost always permanently injured in some way or other. The way the Admiralty treat some of the naval men is most extraordinary, and there was a very queer case at X——shire while I was there. The man in question, James P——, an able seaman, was tried by court-martial while on a foreign station and sentenced to eighteen calendar months' hard labour. While on his way home a native rising occurred in one of our colonies and the man-of-war in which he was being conveyed to England was ordered to proceed forthwith to the colony to assist in quelling the outbreak. On the arrival of the ship at the colony he was given his liberty and allowed to risk his life for his country, and was treated as a free man until his return to England at the conclusion of the war. He had no sooner arrived in an English port than the authorities, discovering that there were still four months of his sentence unexpired, quietly packed him off to prison to complete his sentence. After his arrival at the Xshire prison he sent a petition to the Admiralty representing his case, and asking to be sent back to his ship without undergoing any further punishment, as he had fought and bled for his country in the interim. In due course an answer came down from the Secretary of the Admiralty, saying that it was quite impossible to remit any portion of the sentence, but as it seemed rather a hard case *they would dismiss him from the service at the expiration of his term of imprisonment.* This was the most peculiar way of compensating a man that I, or I expect anybody else, ever heard of, and at first sight it seemed hardly credible, but I carefully inquired into the case and found it was perfectly correct. The man himself told me that he had been born and bred to the sea, and did not know what to do now that they had cast him adrift.

Seamen convicted on foreign stations are very unfairly treated in many ways. As soon as they have been convicted they are sent back to England in the first homeward-bound man-of-war, and are confined in the cells on board, and have to wear irons night and day, the latter being a most useless and unnecessary piece of barbarity, for they are sometimes three and four months before they reach England. On arrival, the prisoner is transferred to the nearest civil prison, and no allowance is made to him there for the three or four months' imprisonment he has undergone on board ship, but he is placed on first class hard labour, only allowed a plank bed to sleep on, and given the same class of diet as though he had only been convicted the previous day. This is manifestly unfair, for if civilians are transferred from one prison to another, their stage card goes with them, and they are placed in whatever class the time they have served in the other prison may entitle them to be in. Seamen ought to be treated in the same way, for their punishment on board ship is, I consider, far more severe than it is while in prison, and a man is not fit for first class hard labour who has been lying in irons night and day for two or three months. Altogether, the poor sailors have a precious hard time of it, and how they ever succeed in getting men to go into the service is the surprise of everybody who knows anything about it.

Meantime, my work in the office had been going quietly on, and proved exceedingly interesting; the only drawback being that while up here I was entirely shut off from the prison, and knew nothing whatever of what might be happening in there during the day. This did not at all suit me, as I wished to know all that was going on, and I knew on good authority that some very queer things went on occasionally. I had now got through nearly half my sentence, and about this time the salt meat episode occurred, and I was ordered back to my cell, "as there was no more work for me to do at present." This was what the Yankees call "rather too thin," as I happened to be just in the middle of a whole lot of work, and the clerk was so much in need of help that they had no sooner got rid of me than another prisoner was ordered up to the office to assist him.

I applied to the governor to know if I had been sent down for any breach of discipline. He said, "Oh no, but I have no more work for you to do at present."

Knowing, as I did, that another man was already employed in the office, I could only conclude that this answer was what is vulgarly called "a good 'un." I was determined to ask as many questions as I could about the matter, so next time the inspector came round I asked him if he had sent me down from the office. He hesitated a moment, and then said, "What's that to you?"

"Well, I thought perhaps you would consider

my case, and give me employment of a similar nature," I answered, "as the close confinement told very much upon my health before."

"You were sentenced to hard labour: I don't call office work hard labour."

"Yes, I know that," I replied; "but the doctor has certified me unfit for first class hard labour, and, besides, I am eligible for employment of trust in the prison, and office work has always been considered to come under that head."

I suppose he could make no answer to this argument, for all he said was, "I don't see why you should be treated differently to anybody else;" and walked off without waiting to hear any more.

I was considerably disappointed by this strategic move on his part, as I should have much liked to ask him why he had allowed me to go on being employed in the office for three consecutive months if it was not hard labour and I had no business to be there.

It was a great nuisance to be shut up again all day in one's cell, but I was afterwards exceedingly glad of it, as I was thus enabled to know all that was going on in the prison for the following six months, and got a thorough insight into the practical working of the prison system. I got the doctor to exempt me from mat-making, and so all I had to do was to pick a little fibre and keep my ears open to all that was going on. I tried to get Duke to take me as his cleaner, but it was no go, he evidently having the greatest contempt for my cleaning capabilities. The billet of cleaner is an eagerly-coveted one, as a cleaner gets any amount of food to eat, and is employed out in the corridors all day. Each warder is allowed to take a prisoner to do the necessary cleaning in his corridor, carry round the food trays, apportion out each man's bread allowance, and perform the thousand and one odd jobs that daily require seeing to. The above duties are all recognized by the authorities; but, in addition, the cleaner has to do a whole lot of work for the warder, which, although strictly prohibited by the regulations, is invariably required of him. For instance, he has to clean the warder's boots, brush his clothes, and, if handy with his needle, mend them also, make his tea the nights that he is on duty, and during the evening clean the wife's and children's shoes ready for the following day. The work all told, however, is a mere nothing to a man accustomed to hard work, and it does not take up more than a quarter of the day to polish the lot off, and the rest of the time is spent in wandering round the corridor making up little imaginary jobs. Every morning the cleaner has to go round cleaning the spy-hole glasses and the handles of the cell-doors, and whilst thus employed holds a short conversation with each prisoner in succession, which is easily done through the glass spy-hole. If the man in the cell has anything very particular to say, he gently scratches the wire-gauze (that is placed over the spy-hole) when he hears the cleaner arrive at his door, and then the latter will discover some grease spots on the slate flooring outside the particular cell, and go and fetch a bucket of water and commence to wash the stains out, a proceeding which takes a considerable time and enables the man inside to say all he wants.

It is in this way that information gets spread all over the prison, and that arrangements are made for dropping notes in chapel or while at exercise. The warders always give their cleaners plenty to eat, so as to prevent their taking the food belonging to the other prisoners while they are engaged in arranging the mess tins on the trays ready for distribution. It is simply awful the quantity of food some of these fellows will consume when first they are appointed cleaners. One fellow, after having had three extra half-pounds of bread at his breakfast, had the same day for his dinner a fourth class dinner, a third class one, and my pudding, so that altogether he had thirty-two ounces of suet pudding, fourteen ounces of potatoes, and ten ounces of bread! and then he actually asked for more! The best billet of all is to get made cleaner to the cook, which simply means preparing the prisoners' meals under the supervision of the cook, and having as much to eat as ever you please—and good food to—boiled meat saved from the amount allowed out for soup, plenty of well-sweetened cocoa, cheese, vegetables, and numerous other perquisites.

Since the government have taken the prisons over, the authorities have introduced the system of only allowing short sentence men to become cleaners. This is an exceedingly stupid and unfair arrangement. Take, for instance, the case of a man sentenced to four months' imprisonment, he does his twenty-eight days on the wheel, and is then taken out as a cleaner, and has far less work to do, and more to eat, than if he were gaining an honest living outside. It completely nullifies the punishment, and only renders the man anxious to get into prison again as soon as the winter comes round or times get hard.

Three months is far too long a time to keep the same man as cleaner, for he gets to know all the ropes, and is continually talking with the other prisoners, and up to all kinds of mischief. The long sentence men mewed up in their cells for twelve, eighteen, and twenty-four months at a stretch, and who really need change of air and employment, are not eligible for these billets. The only long sentence man I knew get made a cleaner while I was at Xshire was a man named Grey, a marine, who had in old days served under the governor, and knew him well. The governor let him go out as a cleaner, although a few weeks later he refused to allow one of the other warders to take out another man (who happened to have exactly the same sentence as Grey, eighteen calendar months), telling him it was against the regulations to take a long sentence man, and that he must look out for some one with a short sentence.

It would be far better in every way, and prevent favouritism, if the commissioners would issue a regulation that all men sentenced to six months and over should, as soon as they were in the fourth stage, be taken out in rotation as cleaners for a week at a time. This would be far better in every way, and by depriving a man of this privilege who was reported while waiting for his turn to come round, the discipline of the prison would be far more easily carried out, as prisoners would be most careful not to forfeit their cleaning week if they could possibly help it. It would also prevent, in a great measure, the constant talking that now goes on between the cleaner and the rest of the prisoners, as a man would have no time to learn all the dodges of the place, and would be afraid to try any pranks.

After about seven months of my sentence had elapsed I became perfectly sickened with the constant sameness of the food, and found it impossible to eat it. I complained to the warder of my corridor, who advised me to see the surgeon on the subject. Acting on his advice, I sent for the latter and laid the matter before him. The doctor luckily happened to be in a great hurry the evening I made the application, and being, in addition, well primed with good whisky, was ready to sign anything he was asked, provided the warder going round with him did not interfere and persuade him not to.

He came bustling down to my cell in a desperate hurry, and said, " Hullo! you want some extra food, don't you?"

"Yes, sir," I said; "I wish you would let me have some cooked beef on Sundays and Wednesdays in lieu of the suet pudding?"

"To be sure, to be sure," he interrupted. "I'll do that for you. You don't want anything else, do you?"

"No, thank you, sir," I answered, and away he hurried, grumbling that he had twelve more men to see and was due home in ten minutes from then.

He did not live far from the prison, and I believe he was back there within the requisite time, so I do not expect he wasted much time in examining the twelve sick men.

The present dietary is totally insufficient for long sentence men. It may be all very well to keep men half starved, who only come in for a week or a fortnight, because by the time they are reduced to the last gasp their sentence expires, and they go out to have a good feed. But to keep men upon the present fourth class diet for twelve months and two years is positive cruelty, and a most false economy. Prisoners break down again and again, unable to bear the heavy strain upon the constitution entailed by this semi-starvation.

Men engaged daily on hard bodily labour must have sufficient food, or no constitution in the world would stand it. It is perfectly useless for the authorities to maintain that the present allowance of food is enough to keep men in health and strength, because, although the dietaries may work admirably in theory, practice distinctly proves that it is not the case.

While engaged balancing the provision books, I carefully went over the list of men for whom the surgeon had ordered extra food, and found that there was not a single man who had been in the prison more than twelve months, that was not in receipt of extra food of some kind or the other.

I had ample proof that the men really did suffer from hunger, and know that after a man had done about six months he was ready to eat anything. I was astonished at the quantity of salt that was consumed, and the continual demand there was for "more salt," and at last inquired what on earth the prisoners did with all they got. I was told that the men were in the habit of eating a spoonful or two after each meal, in order to make themselves exceedingly thirsty, as they were then enabled to fill their stomachs out with a large quantity of water, and, as the man who gave me the information epigrammatically suggested,—

"You cannot feel hungry with a full belly."

On one occasion the cook had made me some paste, and there being considerably more than I wanted, I asked one of the warders if I might have what I required placed in an old mess tin, and then let the rest be thrown away. He gave me the requisite permission, and called to his cleaner to come and find an old tin for me. When the latter saw me preparing to throw away the remainder of the paste he said to the warder,—

"Don't let him waste that, sir; give it to one of the men."

"All right," said the warder, and the cleaner took it from me, and emptying it into a mess tin added a little salt, saying to the warder,—

"Shall I give it to No. 7, sir; he is a very hungry chap?"

"Very well, come along," replied he, and proceeded down the corridor to No. 7's cell.

I followed in their wake, for I was anxious to see the *dénouement*. On arriving at No. 7's door the warder unlocked it, and the cleaner handed in the paste, saying,—

"Here, taste that and see how you like it."

"Ah, thank you," said No. 7, a big, raw-boned Irishman. "I wanted something to eat bad; I have been ill and very sick to-day. That's fine," he continued, after having dipped his fist into the tin and swallowed a handful of the sticky compound it contained.

Later on in the evening I was going round with the warder to light the gas, and as we passed the man's cell he asked him whether he liked what had been given him.

"Have you any more, sir?" was the significant and truly Irish way of answering the question.

It is, however, upon growing lads of sixteen

and seventeen that the unfortunate result of this insufficiency of food is most plainly seen. While I was at Xshire there was a case of the kind. John Jones, aged fifteen, weight 104 pounds, was sentenced to two years' hard labour. He did the first six months of his sentence while the prison was still in the hands of the county authorities, and some interest being taken in his case, he was allowed to go out as cleaner. He was a quiet, clever lad; and when the prisons came under government the warder did all he knew to keep him on as cleaner, and as the boy had got such a long sentence the inspector gave the required permission. Consequently, nearly the whole of this boy's sentence was served by him under the most favourable circumstances; and yet towards the expiration of his sentence he completely lost his health, and although ordered half a pound of mutton daily by the doctor, weighed on discharge, being now seventeen years of age, exactly a quarter of a pound less than he weighed when entering the prison at the age of fifteen. Nor had he increased in height to any appreciable extent, and was able to wear on leaving the clothes he had come to the prison in.

These are actual hard facts that can be verified at any time by simply referring to the Criminal Registry, and must bear a certain amount of weight; for if a boy, owing to the food and confinement, actually stands still as it were for two whole years—years when boys, as a rule, grow faster and fill out more than at any other period—there must be something radically wrong with the present dietary. It is commonly asserted by prison surgeons and officials that prisoners usually gain weight while in prison, and I heard this fact stated more than once at Xshire.

When the Criminal Registry came into my hands I carefully examined into this matter, and found that more than ninety per cent. of the prisoners *lost* weight. There was no possibility of mistake on my part, because the weight of every prisoner, on his arrival at and discharge from the prison, is carefully recorded in the Registry, so that I had only to turn over page after page of it in order to obtain the most satisfactory and conclusive evidence of the real state of affairs.

It is difficult to conceive how the idea ever sprang up in the official mind that men could increase in weight on the present dietary, knowing, as they must, or ought to, that the regulation allowance of food is simply sufficient to sustain life. When once, however, men get a notion of this kind firmly into their heads, it is well-nigh impossible to get it out again. But "facts are stubborn things," and if the commissioners take the trouble to refer to the ample statistics they have at hand, they can easily see how utterly mistaken they are in pompously stating that "prisoners almost invariably increase in weight while in prison." There is no economy in half starving criminals, for on leaving prison they are totally unable to do a day's work (even if they could get it to do), and either find their way into the workhouses and hospitals, or are driven to the committal of fresh crimes through weakness and hunger.

While I was at Xshire an order came down from the commissioners that the box system in the chapel was to be done away with, and the whole chapel arranged in open seats. A couple of extra carpenters were sent for to another prison, and the work of demolition commenced. For a month or more there was no service on week-days, and gradually tier after tier of the boxes disappeared, and rows of fairly comfortable seats, with continuous kneeling boards running in front of them, took the place of our old coffin-like edifices. Much as I disliked the old arrangement I am bound to confess that the new open seats were, in many ways, far more objectionable, and if the boxes were only made (as they easily might be) so as to allow some chance of sitting in comfort, and with sufficient space in front to permit the men to kneel, I am certain that a return to the old system would be decidedly beneficial in every way.

At present the chapel is simply used for conversation, and letter-passing and the constant interchange of news, generally adorned with a liberal allowance of oaths, renders serious attention to the service almost impossible. The governor at Xshire was continually bringing friends into the chapel on Sundays, and the open seats enabled those sitting in the governor's pew to see every prisoner distinctly. I believe it was directly contrary to the regulations, but he did it again and again. It would be far better for all concerned if the authorities were to make it a rule that only the officials themselves (not even their wives and children) were to attend the chapel.

In the old county days the prison was a regular "show place," and old Bob used to take three and four "personally conducted parties" over it every week. And a very pretty sum he made of it; for during the ten years he served under the county he made enough to buy a house, and nearly had a fit when the government regulation came out forbidding strangers to visit the prison.

When nine months of my sentence had expired, I began to suffer very much from the close confinement, and became perfectly lightheaded at times. In addition to this, my eyes, owing to the continual glare of the whitewashed walls, became in such a state that the doctor forbade my using them in any way whatever. I was now fairly stranded, and as it was perfectly dreadful to be sitting day after day with my hands before me, I determined to try and get the doctor to let me be employed about the corridor, as that would be a great relief to both my eyes and head. First of all, however, I thought I would lay the matter before the governor; but as he did not go round the following morning I seized the opportunity of his going round with a stranger in the afternoon, and said,—

"If you please, sir, my health is very bad, may I exercise in the corridor?"

"Yes, if the doctor orders it," he replied, and passed on.

That evening I sent for the doctor and laid the matter before him. He carefully examined my eyes, stethoscoped my lungs, and then said,—

"Want to go out in the corridor, do you? To be sure, to be sure. I'll make an order."

The following day I asked the warder if any order had come down from the office about my being about in the corridor, and he told me that the governor had expressly ordered that I was *not* to be allowed out in the corridor. I thought that this was rather funny, for if the doctor orders a prisoner anything, the governor has no power whatever to interfere; so I determined to send for the doctor again. When I saw him he informed me that he had seen the governor the previous evening, and strongly recommended my being allowed to exercise in the corridor, and finished up with,—

"It will be quite right when you see the governor on his rounds to-morrow; he will give the necessary orders."

The governor came round the next day, but did not say a word; so the morning following I stopped him and asked the question.

"The doctor only advised extra exercise," he said.

"Oh, but the doctor assured me last night that he had had an interview with you," I replied, "and had strongly advised my being allowed to exercise in the corridor."

He paused a moment or two in evident confusion, and then said,—

"I particularly disapprove of anybody airing in the corridor."

"But when I applied to you the other day, sir," I answered, "you told me to apply to the doctor."

He hummed and hawed, and, after a good deal of hesitation, finally said "he would see the doctor again on the subject."

This interview took place on a Saturday, and the following Monday the governor stopped at my cell as he was going his rounds, and said,—

"I have seen the doctor about you, and he tells me there is no physical reason why you should exercise in the corridor, and as I greatly disapprove of anybody's exercising in the corridor, if you require any extra airing you must take it outside."

"But there are other prisoners who exercise in the corridor, sir," I replied.

"No there are not," he said shortly, and commenced to move on; but I was getting what the Yankees call "considerably riled," and was not going to let him depart with a flat denial of that kind.

"Why, there is No. 35 B exercising in the corridor," I said; "and 37 A always took his exercise in the corridor all the time he was here."

He looked rather nonplussed at this, and after a moment's hesitation said,—

"Well, that I know nothing about."

Of course, if he did not know what was being done in the prison, there was no use continuing the discussion, so I gave it up for the time being.

I was not at all satisfied about the matter, for I knew that the governor had no right whatever to have rescinded, or induced the doctor to rescind, the order that had been made for me to have exercise in the corridor.

Under the government regulations a prisoner has the right of sending a petition to the Home Secretary if he considers that he is being improperly treated, though, of course, it is a serious thing to take the responsibility of doing so, as a commission would be sent down to examine into the whole case, whatever it was, and there would be altogether a tremendous fuss.

I considered the matter for several days, for I was greatly tempted to send up a petition, knowing how distinctly it was laid down in the regulations that anything ordered for a prisoner by the medical officer of the prison was to be immediately given him, and that the governor had no power whatever to interfere about anything that the doctor might order a man.

I took advice on the matter, and was strongly urged to abandon the idea. The arguments used were—

1st. That I had only got a very short time longer to serve, and that it was not worth while.

2nd. That things would be made very unpleasant for me if I did.

3rd. That while I should only be able to tell my story publicly to the commissioners who would be sent down, the governor would be able to make all sorts of statements that I should know nothing about.

4th. That whatever the Home Office officials *thought*, they would feel bound to support the governor; and,—

5th. That Sir Edmund du Cane was reported to be such a "cranky fellow that you didn't know where to take him, and there was no telling what fuss and bother he might not make."

Notwithstanding all these arguments, I was exceedingly loth to give up my intention; but I finally decided that "the game was not, perhaps, after all, worth the candle."

Just about this time a medical man (I understood he was one of the Millbank surgeons) was sent down by the Home Office to report on the health of the prisoners, and examine the sanitary arrangements of the prison. If his examination of the Xshire prison was a sample of the way he performed his duty, the Home Office authorities might just as well keep their money in their pockets. He came into the prison about two o'clock, accompanied by the governor and chief warder, and, commencing on the south side of the corridor, went into all the cells where there were prisoners, until he reached my door. Here there was a brief consultation held between him and the governor, and finally the governor gave orders that I was to be inspected too. I had heard all the banging of doors, and this whispered conversation outside my cell, and immediately concluded that it was one of the visiting justices wandering round to while away an hour.

When my door was opened and I saw a young well-dressed man with a most irreproachable tall hat, I felt quite satisfied that my suspicions were correct, and when after a moment's hesitation he mildly simpered out, "What's your name? are you well?" and on his questions being answered passed on to the next cell the evidence was conclusive, for these were just the kind of idiotic questions the justices generally did ask. If I had only known that he was a medical man inquiring into the health of the prisoners I should have had a good deal to say to him, but I naturally imagined that it would be perfectly useless to give a graphic description of the state of my health to a visiting justice, and so lost my opportunity.

On quitting my cell he decided that he had sufficiently examined the prison, and so departed with the governor. The efficacy of his examination may be gathered from the following facts.

He commenced, as I have already stated, on the south side of C corridor, and came as far as my cell; he would thus pass seventeen cells inclusive of mine. Of these seventeen, five would be vacant, their occupants being engaged, three as cleaners and one at the loom, while the owner of the fifth was lying dead in the hospital. He would thus have examined twelve prisoners in this corridor, while the rest of the corridors were left entirely unnoticed.

Now just as it happened there were no men ill on my side of the corridor, but if he had taken the trouble to go round the other side he would have found three men ill, two so seriously as to be obliged to keep their hammocks. When a medical man is sent down he might just as well examine the prison thoroughly, and each prisoner ought to be told that the visitor was a surgeon from the Home Office, and then if they had any complaints to make they would have an opportunity of making them.

There was a very sad case came under my notice towards the end of my time. It was that of a boy of eighteen, who was sent to the prison to await trial on a charge of felony. The unfortunate creature was evidently what is popularly called "soft," and the doctor was ordered to examine him and see whether he was sufficiently *compos mentis* to plead. On the night of the examination in question the old doctor had had a glass or two of his favourite beverage, and the whole proceeding was ludicrous beyond description. The doctor leant against one side of the little table in the cell and the idiot against the other; every now and then the doctor would lurch over towards him with a Prayer Book in his outstretched hand, and ask him whether he saw it and could read it. The poor idiot was frightened out of his life, and could not make head or tail of the whole proceeding, but was ready to say or do anything. Ultimately the doctor decided that he was quite sane enough to know what he was about, and the boy was accordingly tried in due course at the Quarter Sessions. He was convicted and sentenced to six months' hard labour. I imagine that the boy was simply soft, that is to say, there was no actual madness, but he was an unreasoning kind of animal; and when it was explained to him that he was going to be locked up for six months, and he found himself back in the prison with the fact staring him in the face, he became desperate and tried to rush out of the receiving ward. Of course he was promptly collared and placed in a cell. He thought this bad enough, but when he was ordered to take his clothes off and have a cold bath it was indeed "the last straw," and becoming perfectly frantic he howled and yelled and rushed about like a perfect maniac. With considerable trouble he was eventually washed and conducted to a cell. He no sooner found himself alone than he got hold of the bed straps and proceeded to try and hang himself, and would undoubtedly have succeeded in his attempt had not one of the warders caught him in the act. The matter was reported to the governor, and orders were sent out that he was to be taken down to the receiving ward again and placed in a cell situated there that was specially fitted up with a view to frustrating any attempt at self-destruction. The cell in question is denuded of all furniture, and prisoners occupying it had a plank bed and bedding passed into them at night and taken away again in the morning. There was no gas in the cell, but there was a small thick round of plate glass in the lower part of the door, and a movable gas burner in the corridor with a reflector attached to it was placed opposite this by the warder, and in this way a certain amount of light found its way into the cell. The cells in this part of the receiving ward were terribly dark during the day, for the wheelhouse ran along parallel with the windows and blocked out every gleam of sunshine, and between next to no daylight during the day and the above described gleam of gaslight at night, they were hardly the kind of places to be considered desirable residences. Here the unfortunate idiot was located, and left day after day week after week in semi-darkness without any employment and with absolutely nothing whatever to employ his mind. It would have been quite enough to drive the sanest man in the world raving mad in a couple of months, and think what it must have been to this poor soft-brained boy. At first he used to howl and scream for an hour at a time, nothing would pacify him; then after three weeks he took to simply moaning like some dumb beast in mortal agony, and then after another week or so he became perfectly quiet and used to lie day after day stretched on the floor in a half stupefied condition. This state of things went on for about a month, and then the doctor decided that the boy was insane, the necessary papers were signed, and the unfortunate youth transferred to the county lunatic asylum to live at the expense of the ratepayers for the rest of his life.

The miserable boy was not even allowed to have the exercise he was entitled to, because, on the one or two occasions that old Bob let him out, he lay on the grass and cried when he found that it was impossible for him to run home; and as Bob considered this detrimental to prison discipline and good order, he took the matter into his own hands, and did not let the boy out any more. It was a wretched, cruel case, and reflected the greatest discredit on every one of the higher officials of the prison.

It is a most extraordinary thing to me what induced the authorities to continue the use of treadwheels in the prisons? They are not the slightest use in any way. They only waste an enormous amount of valuable labour, which, if properly applied, would very soon make the prisons self-supporting. It is no punishment to a man accustomed to hard work, and I have known case after case of men applying for leave to go on the wheel sooner than stay doing nothing in their cells. I questioned several prisoners on the subject, and invariably got the same reply, that " it was hard work for the first day or two, until you got into the knack of it, and then it was easy enough." I used to go into the wheelhouse sometimes and watch the men at work, and on two or three occasions I got up and tried it myself, and although I must frankly own that I should not have cared to do a day's work on it myself, I became quite convinced that it was simply a question of practice, and no punishment whatever to an habitual criminal, or indeed to any one accustomed to hard out-door labour.

My time was now rapidly drawing to a close, and the days seemed terribly long, but a slight additional impetus was given them as a new case, or rather an old case in a new phase, came under my notice, and occupied my attention for a few days.

An habitual criminal named Colls, who had been convicted again and again, until both his health and intellect had completely given way under the incessant confinement and short commons, had once more just completed his sentence (twelve months' hard labour). The day before he was liberated he was told by both the surgeon and warders that the best thing he could do was to go straight to the union, as he was quite incapable of doing any work. Three days after his discharge he was back again in prison, with one month's hard labour for begging. Old Bob, as usual, never took the trouble to mention the case to the doctor, and so Colls was duly certified fit for first class labour, and turned out to do his eight hours on the wheel. A few days of this very soon did for him, and he became so ill that the doctor ordered him to be moved into hospital, and recommended his release and removal to the union. The man was duly released, and on arriving at the union the authorities there decided that he was an idiot, he was undoubtedly not in his right mind, and informed the manager of the county lunatic asylum that they intended sending him there. This was strongly protested against by the asylum authorities, and there was every chance of a very pretty quarrel, when Colls took the matter into his own hands and died. I made some very careful inquiries as to why the man had not gone to the union at first as he had been advised, and was told that he had gone up to the superintendent of police and tried to get an order for admission to the workhouse, but was refused, and told to go about his business. Now this man being perfectly incapable, both mentally and physically, of doing any work, had absolutely no choice but to starve, steal, or beg. Of the ten shillings that he had received on his discharge he had spent four shillings the first day, and the remaining six were stolen from him at the place where he slept. This is only one case out of many. There are, I believe, hundreds of such cases occurring every week in England.

Slowly, slowly the days crept along till my last day in prison arrived, and I received orders from the governor to go down to the receiving ward and select what clothes I wished to wear, from the portmanteau of things I had stowed away in the store-room.

The eventful morning came at last, and having received permission from the governor to leave the prison at six o'clock in the morning (prisoners are usually liberated at ten, unless they have a long journey to take, and are unable to reach their homes if kept till that hour), I bade an early farewell to Xshire prison and its many trials and troubles; and though on entering it I fancied that I had lost everything that made life worth living for, I found long before my time was served that my loss was as nothing when compared with the " pearl of great price " that it had been permitted me to find, through the discipline, the reflection, the solitude, and suffering of my prison life. Looking back upon the fearful peril from which I was snatched, remembering how utter was the wreck, I can indeed say, with humble, deep-felt gratitude, " He doeth all things well."

And now I shall soon lay aside my pen, and let these pages go forth with their many blemishes, their many defects, but still with an earnest, hearty hope that by their means some of the abuses of our present prison system may be stamped out, some of the unnecessary cruelties prevented in the future, and some better mode of reclaiming criminals be adopted.

In conclusion, let me urge most strongly the great desirability of keeping apart first offenders and habitual criminals. This admixture is the foulest blot of all upon the present system, and the one easiest of removal. There is no reason whatever why one corridor in each prison should not be kept for first offenders, another for those previously convicted, and a third for the so-called habitual criminal. Let the rules and dietaries be also drawn up in accordance with this arrangement, the regulation becoming more stringent, and the food more scanty, as men proved their determination to continue in crime. Above all, let the authorities try by every means in their power to find employment for those first offenders who are willing to work hard and try and regain an honest name.

Lastly, let me say that in whatever I have written concerning the officials of the Xshire prison I have honestly striven to "set down naught in malice and to extenuate nothing."

THE END.

LONDON:
PRINTED BY GILBERT AND RIVINGTON, LIMITED
ST. JOHN'S SQUARE.

www.ingramcontent.com/pod-product-compliance
Lightning Source LLC
Chambersburg PA
CBHW032134230426
43672CB00011B/2334